THE BOOK ON MOTORCYCLE CAMPING

by

The Lonesome Hillbilly

Dedicated to

William S. Harley
and
Arthur Davidson

Who unlocked the door
So we could get out

Copyright© 2017 The Lonesome Hillbilly

Photographs and Cover Art by The Lonesome Hillbilly

Contents

1	**Introduction**
2	**The Motorcycle**
2	The Bike
4	Tires
6	Gear for the Bike
8	Tips for Mountain and Dirt Roads
11	**Gear for You**
12	List Section
15	Detail Section
27	Tool Kit
31	Cooking Kit
34	Clothes Kit
38	Sewing Kit
40	First Aid Kit
41	Emergency Kit
49	Stowage
54	Water
56	**Camping**
56	Where to go
58	The Campsite
59	Campfires
59	Fire Safety
60	About Firewood
62	Gathering Firewood
65	Preparing the the Ground
66	Laying out the Fire
67	Lighting the Fire
68	Fire for Cooking
69	Fire for Warmth

69	Winter Camping
72	Camping Tips and Tricks
72	Ticks
72	Insect Repellent
73	Mosquito Bites
74	Scorpions
74	Rattlesnakes
75	Other Venomous Critters
75	Passes
75	Hygiene
76	Cat-holes and Slit Trenches
77	Keeping Cool
78	Keeping Warm
79	Keeping Things Cool
79	Multi-Use Gear
79	Things You Need to Know

81   Campfire Cooking

81	Camp Stove vs. Camp Fire
83	Boiling and Simmering
83	Frying and Sauteeing
84	Roasting
84	Planking
84	Baking
85	High Altitude Cooking
86	Boiling and Simmering
86	Grilling, Roasting and Broiling
88	Deep-Fat Frying
88	Slow Cooker
88	Pressure Cooker
89	Baking
91	Cookware
91	Pots and Pans
91	Seasoning Cast Iron
93	Cleaning and Care of Cast Iron
94	Utensils

94	About Food
94	Storing Food in Camp
98	Spoilage
99	Dry Stuff
101	Recipes
101	Bannock
102	Corn Bread
102	Steamed Rice
103	Corn Meal Mush
103	Apple Topping (for pancakes, etc.)
103	Black-Eye Peas, or any dry beans
104	Grilled Cheese Sandwiches
104	Beef & Beans
105	Simple Improvised Recipes

106   Paying For It

106	Bike Maintenance
107	Registration
107	Insurance
107	Gas
107	Food
108	Camping Fees
108	Replacement
108	Clothes
108	Repairs

110   Glossary

114   About the Author

Chant-Pagan
English Irregular Discharged
by Rudyard Kipling

Me that 'ave been what I've been --
Me that 'ave gone where I've gone --
Me that 'ave seen what I've seen --
'Ow can I ever take on
With awful old England again,
An' 'ouses both sides of the street,
And 'edges two sides of the lane,
And the parson an' gentry between,
An' touchin' my 'at when we meet --
Me that 'ave been what I've been?

. . . . .

I will arise an' get 'ence --
I will trek South and make sure
If it's only my fancy or not
That the sunshine of England is pale,
And the breezes of England are stale,
An' there's somethin' gone small with the lot.
For I know of a sun an' a wind,
An' some plains and a mountain be'ind,
An' some graves by a barb-wire fence,
An' a Dutchman I've fought 'oo might give
Me a job where I ever inclined
To look in an' offsaddle an' live
Where there's neither a road nor a tree --
But only my Maker an' me,
And I think it will kill me or cure,
So I think I will go there an' see.

Introduction

This book is not about motorcycles, and it is not about biking. It is about camping, on, with, and by means of a motorcycle. It is about what may be the most free and open lifestyle possible today. Today's motorcycle camper can go wherever he chooses whenever he wants, and still live in comfort. (Granted, the stay-at-home would not think this life comfortable, but that is exactly why he *is* a stay-at-home.) We are the heirs of the Rocky Mountain fur trappers, by way of the mid-twentieth-century backpackers. By means of the bike, we can skip through a hundred or two miles of tamed land to get to the true wilds, then live there as long as we please before moving on to a new horizon.

I assume you already know how to ride; if you don't, take a good basic riding course, then ride a lot for several months before heading out. The only "how to ride" data included here is specifically for the mountains and deserts, things a city or highway rider normally would not need.

While this book is intended for the motorcycle camper, most of the data is equally applicable if you backpack or travel by car or even RV. Picking a campsite, gathering firewood, building a fire, cooking – these apply to everyone. Most of the gear is also universal. The main difference in the styles of camping is how much gear you *can* take with you. But let me caution you: Don't pack something just because you can. In general, the less gear you have, the better.

If you are only out for a weekend, you do not really need this book. If you are out for a couple of weeks, some of this data will be overkill. But if you plan to spend a whole season on the road, or go full-time, this data should make it fairly easy to start. This is how I do it all year, year after year, hopefully for the rest of my life. This is how I live the dream.

The Motorcycle

The Bike

I do not expect you will buy a new bike for camping, but maybe you will. These are the features to look for, and the reasons they are good, and the trade-offs. Maybe you will find your bike is not suitable, maybe you can modify it, maybe you will decide to get a different one. But bear in mind, while I have ridden sports bikes and street bikes and dirt bikes, I have only camped on a cruiser. I am no expert on the other styles.

A large part of this is personal taste. I have not ridden all makes, and only have significant experience on Hondas and Harleys, so I cannot say much about it. The only bad bikes I know of are the AMF Harleys, which were butchered for profit. Bikes from that period are trash; they require a lot of maintenance, and break down frequently. More recent Harleys are good. The Harley has a mystique, a symbolism that many bikers value. The bikes and parts for them are more expensive, and in my experience they need more care and maintenance, but there are Harley dealers and service shops everywhere. When you are camping in the mountains or the desert, you *need* a dependable ride. At the least, a breakdown will ruin your vacation; at worst, it will kill you.

Hondas and Honda parts are much less expensive. There are fewer shops (if there is only one shop in a town, it will be Harley-Davidson; count on it), but they require a lot less maintenance. In my experience, if you take proper care of a Honda bike, mainly changing the oil every three or four thousand miles, and doing the recommended maintenance actions, it just does not break down. On the road, that is perhaps the most important consideration.

The Lonesome Hillbilly

So, which make and model you ride depends entirely on what you like, what you feel good with. I ride a Honda VTX 1300, and it is hands down the best bike I have ever ridden. The following points are what I have learned from experience, and apply to any bike at all:

- A cruiser or tour bike is more comfortable for long trips. You can sit in several different positions, which can be important when you ride more than a hundred miles.
- The bigger the bike, the more you can carry, but the smaller the bike, the easier (and safer) it is to ride on dirt roads, especially when rutted. There are places you can get to on a smaller bike that you simply cannot take a heavy cruiser.
- Shaft drive is less likely to break down than chain or belt drives. If you have chain or belt drive, carry a repair kit.
- Solid wheels with tubeless tires allow quick flat repair.
- A windscreen is much more comfortable, and on faster highways will increase your duration a lot.
- The larger the gas tank, the better, especially in the Western deserts and mountains where it may be a hundred miles or more to the next gas station. Know how many miles you can go before switching to reserve gas, and how far you can go on reserve. Test it by carrying a can of gas and running the tank dry. Also be aware that mileage changes with speed and with wind conditions. I once made a two hundred mile trip there and back, head wind going and tail wind returning, and got 50 MPG with the wind, 30 against it. Your best mileage will be at the slowest speed you can go in your highest gear. At 35, I approach 50 MPG. At 80, I only get 30 MPG.
- A sissy bar makes it easier to secure your gear. Also a cargo rack behind the sissy bar.
- Freeway bars make it easier to right the bike if you drop it; otherwise, you may have to unload first.

- Big mirrors with wide view are preferable, especially since you will usually be riding slower than the rest of the traffic. The higher and wider they are set, the better you will see past your load. Get mirrors with long brackets.
- Fenders are necessary, especially on dirt and gravel roads. You don't want sand, dust and mud in your face, or on your gear.
- Quiet pipes are best. You can hear the world around you better, and you are less likely to annoy other campers, especially if you arrive late or leave early.
- Get the loudest horn you can, so you can scare the cagers who don't see you.
- A water-cooled motor is best, and is vital for desert travel.
- Get comfortable handlebars. What is right for me may not be right for you, but I like the grips to be six or eight inches below my shoulders, and at such an angle that when going straight, my wrists are not bent more than half an inch outwards. The grips slope slightly downwards, maybe ten or twenty degrees. I have found this configuration is most comfortable when riding for hours.
- A Heel-Toe shift allows quicker and easier shifting, and you may shift a lot on mountain roads.
- Foot plates or floorboards are more comfortable and restful on long rides because you can shift your foot position.
- Kickstands sometimes allow a pretty extreme lean angle; it may be too much for a loaded bike. Consider an after-market kickstand that keeps the bike more upright.
- If the bike has a cruise control, great. If not, get a throttle lock.
- If the battery is not easily accessible when the bike is loaded, rig pigtail wires, *thick* ones, on the battery cables so you can connect for jump starts (giving and receiving) without unloading your gear. Carry bike jumper cables.

- A kick starter can be very valuable.
- If your bike does not have a cigarette lighter, add one. Get a USB-to-lighter adapter; that should serve for all of your electronics. You can also get an inverter that fits in the lighter and outputs A/C, if you have anything that only charges from house current, but I have never found one that works on a motorcycle if the motor is not running.
- Get tough heavy-duty tires rated about 80 MPH; you won't be going any faster. You will be riding on dirt and gravel roads, and will likely need the extra strength.
- I will not have ABS (Automated Braking System), which works both front and rear brakes regardless of which brake lever you use. It is good for city and highway use, but on mountain roads which often have gravel or sand on the pavement, and especially on dirt and gravel roads, it is dangerous. ABS denies you control and can cause you to drop the bike. If my bike had ABS, I would disconnect it.

Tires

You need good tires, ones that will wear long and can stand up to rocks and rough roads. You do *not* need high-speed tires or whitewalls. Do replace them well before they go bald, because the thinner tread is more liable to punctures from sharp rocks, and you never know when the mountains will drop rain on the road. Take care of them. Avoid rocks and sticks, and ride slowly on rough roads; you can safely roll over a rock at 10 MPH that would slash the tire at 40. Avoid skidding when braking, and never lay rubber when you can avoid it.

In the chapter on Stowage, I write about extending tire life by making the tire wear uniform. Regardless of theory, that technique works for me, and has extended tire life.

Keep the tires inflated to the recommended (not maximum) pressure; they are designed to give maximum performance and longevity when at the recommended pressure. Under-inflated tires create excess heat from the rubber flexing, which damages the belts of radial tires. Over-inflated tires will wear more on the center; that just means there will still be tread on the edges when the center is so worn you must replace the tire. What you are after is *uniform* wear, left, right and center. Some say over-inflated tires also give better gas mileage, but in my experience, it is not significant. Of course, I also change altitude a lot, and that skews the results; a tire inflated to 32 PSI at 5,000 feet will be at 34 PSI at 10,000, then back at 32 when I come back down.

You could go to the Dark Side, buying auto tires that fit your wheels. Auto tires last a *lot* longer than motorcycle tires, but they are flat, not rounded, so bike handling is very different. I have read a lot about their pros and cons, and they clearly are the cheaper way to go. But I have read nothing about their use on heavily loaded bikes, and I do not trust the idea. Your choice.

Gear for the Bike

- On longer trips, carry your bike's Service Manual.
- Oil filter for your bike. Just about any bike service shop can change your oil, but even one that specializes in your brand may not have the right filter in stock. Carry one or two yourself, just in case.
- A sheepskin (real or fake) car seat cover makes a great pad for the saddle. By folding it in different ways, you can change the shape of the saddle to give your butt relief.
- Carry a plate, four to six inch diameter, to put under the kickstand on sand or soft soil. It can be a thin flat rock, a piece of plywood, metal, strong plastic, whatever. A strong plastic coffee cup saucer works well. It should be

tied to the bike so you can drop it and use your toe to maneuver it into place without dismounting.
- Bike bell: Get a good solid bell, one to two inches high. Brass is best, pewter is no good; it needs to make a good solid ring. Attach it as low as you can on the frame, so the road gremlins will drop to the road when they fall out.
- You can get a small solar panel, about 1 1/2 watts, for about fifteen dollars. It plugs into the cigarette lighter, and can keep your battery topped off. You probably won't need this if you do not charge things from the bike.
- The best gear for a flat battery is a jump-start kit. It contains a lithium battery about 6"x4"x1" and clip cables to attach to the bike battery. If you have pig-tailed the bike battery, you can do a jump-start in two or three minutes. The battery can be kept charged by solar panel, by your bike battery, or by house current. It also has outlets for charging electronic devices. I have seen them for sixty to two hundred dollars. Mine was sixty dollars, and works very well. If you do not carry a jump-starter, park well up a good slope wherever possible so you can do a pop-start. Unload the bike before doing a pop-start, especially if you are on a dirt road; it is easy to lose your balance when the rear wheel skids.
- Snow chains are a good idea. You should avoid snow whenever possible, but be ready for it. Mountain storms can brew up very quickly, and at higher altitudes you may get hit with a snow storm in July. I have. If there is threat of snow, you will not be allowed to cross some passes if you do not have chains. You probably will never need them, but if you plan to ride the higher mountains, you should carry them.

Tips for Mountain and Dirt Roads

- Take it slowly. The extra weight of your gear means you will slip on curves at lower speed. You also have to stay alert for rocks, gravel, sand and landslides; they are common in the hills. Besides, you will see and hear a lot more at lower speeds. The idea is to enjoy the ride for its own sake. If all you want is to reach your destination, you might as well drive a cage.
- Watch for animals, who usually panic and freeze at the sight of your bike. If you hit a deer, it could kill you. If you see a critter in the road, slow down as quickly as you safely can. I do not try to avoid the animal, except at night; I aim straight for it. At night, aim to miss behind it, because if they do move, it will usually be forward. During the day, the animal will usually freeze till you are almost on it, then dash away at the last quarter second, but it may go in either direction. The only times I have ever hit one were when I was trying to miss it; as often as not, it jumped right in front of me; I have never run over a critter I was aiming at. But if you do hit one, please, go back and make sure it is dead. Don't leave it suffering.
- You will often be on long downslopes. Learn engine braking and use it when possible to avoid overheating and burning out your brakes. Basically, you throttle down, part or all of the way, while leaving the gears engaged, or after downshifting. It does wear the gears, but only on the backs of the teeth; it will not wear out your transmission. It can wear out your clutch if you ride it. Don't pop the clutch, because you may cause the rear wheel to skid, but do release the clutch fully as soon as you can. Some towns ban engine braking. They usually refer to jake brakes on diesel trucks, but it is best to play it safe and use your regular brakes in town.

- On dirt roads and on curves, and on pavement when there is dirt or gravel on the road, avoid using the front brake at all, because you can very easily skid the front wheel and low-side the bike; the slightest bit of slippage can cause the front wheel to leap out from under you and drop the bike. In general, I use only the front brake to slow on straight asphalt or concrete. Everywhere else, I use only the rear brake. This keeps the wear on the brake pads more uniform. I only use both brakes when I need to slow or stop quickly.
- On curves, the rear wheel can also skid when you brake or if you enter a curve too fast, especially when all of your gear is loaded. Take it slowly.
- Some will tell you that engine braking will not cause your rear wheel to skid. This is just not true, especially on dirt or gravel.
- Deep gravel provides little support, and will allow the front wheel to slip sideways, just like braking on a curve. The only worse road is one with deep ruts.
- Ruts can jerk your wheel to the side and drop the bike. Large rocks and potholes can do the same. Avoid them whenever possible. If you cannot avoid them, go slowly. In big deep ruts, go at a walking pace with your feet positioned to catch the bike. As you gain experience, you may go faster, but be cautious. Ridges, bumps, washboarding and potholes are common; watch for them and take them slowly. If your load is not securely tied, the bumping can make it shift and mess up your balance.
- When riding on washboard, stop and check your load periodically, say every hour or so, to make sure nothing is shaking loose.
- If a paved road has rocks, gravel or sand on it, treat it as you would a dirt road.
- Fine gravel on pavement can make your foot slip and drop you.

- On blind mountain curves, ride slowly near the center of the road on right-turning curves, so you can see farther and can dodge either way, or near the right edge on left-turning curves. You can see farther ahead so you have more time to react to oncoming traffic. *Always* expect oncoming traffic.
- In areas where logging is in progress, stay alert for logging trucks. They often go very fast. The drivers are usually very good, and will not hit you, but they can startle you into overreacting.
- If the wind is gusty, slow down a bit and try to stay near the center of the road, away from cliffs and drop-offs.
- Take it slowly if you are riding in a rainy area or on dirt and gravel roads. With your added load, you increase the risk of losing traction in water, and of blowouts from sharp rocks.
- If you ride dusty areas a lot, check the air filter frequently. Most brands can be washed out. The easiest way is to vacuum them, sucking the dirt out from the same side it came in. Washing with water is most effective; just run water in the outlet side. Or you can dip the filter in soapy water to flush it. If you use water, let the filter dry *completely* before reinstalling it.
- As a general rule, I always take mountain roads pretty slowly, so I can look around and enjoy the view. After all, that is why we go there. Be courteous to the drivers behind you; pull over when you can and let them get by.
- You will only rarely be needing to get somewhere quickly. Take your time and enjoy the ride. Stop to look and take pictures when you see a particularly beautiful scene. Ride easily so you are not tense or worn out when you reach your destination. It is a lot more fun this way.

Gear for You

What gear you carry is entirely up to you, to fit your tastes and needs and capacity. If you are only going for a weekend, you need little, and the hardship of forgetting something won't last long. If you are going for a couple of weeks, you can skip a lot of gear; if you will be eating only canned food and sandwiches, you can skip the whole cooking kit, except a can opener and a spoon. I have lists here for long-term camping, months at least. I camp year-round, so I carry everything. These lists are generally what I carry. The gear weighs about 150 pounds, the largest part being thirty pounds of canvas tent. I usually only carry about three days worth of food, because grocery stores are so common. I will make camp, then go buy enough food for my stay.

Your bike has a recommended load capacity. This is the weight of everything not the bike. Do not exceed this weight, but do not be afraid of it, either; the bike is designed to carry that load. Properly stowed, it is much like carrying a passenger, one who is well trained and never moves. My bike has a recommended load of 400 pounds. My 220 plus the 150 pounds of gear adds up to 370, well within the limit.

First is a list of all items, including "kits" and their contents; it is useful as a checklist for when you are packing. Then there is a detail section describing most items in the lists, in the same order as on the lists. From the details you can decide whether or not you want to carry it.

This list assumes one person traveling alone. If there are two or more people in the party, many items need not be duplicated in each persons load. These I mark with an asterisk (*). Divide these up so each person carries part of them.

List Section

- Gas can
- Saddle bags
- Duffel bags and cloth sacks
- Tank bag
- Sleeping bags
- Water jugs
- *Water purifier
- *Tent with groundcloth
- *Rope
- *Axe, hatchet or machete
- *Shovel
- Pocket knife and sheath knife
- Tarp for the load
- *Grommet kit
- Straps and caribiner clips
- *Map case
- Camp chair
- Toilet paper
- Solar shower
- Notebooks and pens
- Camera
- Binoculars
- Canteen for hiking and riding
- *Radio
- Sunscreen

Emergency Kit (covered in a chapter of its own.)

Tool Kit
- *Standard bike tools for your model bike
- *Puncture repair kit and air pump
- *Duck tape

- *Baling wire
- *WD-40
- *3-in-1 oil
- *Knife sharpener
- *Spare fuses (at least three of each size)
- *Spare light bulbs (at least one of each size you use)
- Spare control cables and tubes
- *Shorty hammer
- *Diagonal cutters, for the baling wire
- Boiled Linseed Oil
- Neatsfoot Oil

Cooking Kit
- *Camp stove
- *Big pot with lid
- *Small pot with lid
- *Cast iron frying pan, 8"
- *Cast iron frying pan, 10" with lid
- *Meat thermometer
- *Long spoon, fork, ladle and spatula
- *Cutting board, 7"x9"
- Bowl
- Fork and spoon
- *Salt, pepper and spices
- *Jars for oils
- *Paper towels
- *Dish soap
- *Body soap
- *Scrubber
- *Bags for big pot and frying pans
- *Dutch oven
- *Grill
- *Coffee pot

Clothes Kit
- Boots
- Shoes
- Sandals
- Long pants, 3
- Short pants
- Long sleeve shirt, 2
- T-shirts, 3
- Underpants, 4
- Woolen long underwear, 2
- Thermal long underwear, 1
- Socks, 4
- Bandannas, 3
- Belt
- Towel
- Rain gear (jacket, pants, boot covers)
- Helmet with visor
- Helmet liner
- Sunglasses
- Riding gloves
- Chaps
- Kidney belt
- Work gloves
- Hat, wide brim
- Bag for dirty clothes
- *Laundry soap

Sewing Kit
- *Needles, various sizes
- *Fine thread
- *Heavy thread
- *Stitch-awl with waxed thread
- *Safety pins, various sizes

- *Scissors
- *Measuring tape

First Aid Kit
- *Band-aids
- *Large sterile gauze pads
- *Adhesive tape
- *Ace bandages, ankle and rib sizes
- *Iodine
- *Cotton swabs

Gear for the Bike
This list was detailed in an earlier chapter. I include it here as a checklist.
- Service Manual
- Oil filter
- Sheepskin seat cover
- Kickstand plate
- Bike bell
- Solar panel
- Jump-start kit
- Snow chains

This may look like a lot of gear. Well, it is. But it weighs less than 150 pounds, though on the bike, it looks like a lot more. Properly stowed, it is safe and comfortable.

Detail Section

Gas can
Your mileage on mountain and dirt roads will vary from street and highway use. Gas stations may be far apart, and traffic rare.

Always carry a gallon can of spare gas. It is also needed if you have a gasoline camp stove. Every month or so, empty it into your tank when you gas up, and fill it with fresh gas. Carry the can where you can get at it easily (without unpacking), and well away from pipes and motor. Note that this is *not* marked as a "group" item. If one person needs extra gas, it is likely the others will, too.

Saddle bags
These should be the biggest you can get. I made a set by cutting an 18" diameter, four-foot long Outdoor Gear duffel bag in half, sewing a double layer of canvas on each open end, then attaching (very strongly) the tops and inner sides from my old (and worn out) commercial bags. Thus I had good solid rigging for hanging them across the saddles, and more than three times the capacity of any commercial set. All of my heavy gear goes in them (see chapter on Stowing).

Duffel bags and cloth sacks
I carry two very large duffels. Obviously, it is easier and safer to strap on one or two bags than eight or ten. Get the largest that will fit, measuring from the outer edges of your saddlebags, and from the sissy bar to your back. On my bike, that is forty inches long by fifteen inches wide. Rather than just dump everything into a pair of duffels, I have smaller sacks, one for clothes, one for cooking gear, and so on. The sacks go in the duffels, and I can easily find what I am after by grabbing the correct sack, rather than grubbing through the whole duffel. Sportsman's Guide is an excellent source of camping gear, and they have a lot of military surplus gear at good prices. I bought an assortment of sacks from them for my gear.

Tank bag
Good place to carry rain gear and other stuff you are likely to need on the road. Carry it here so you don't have to unpack to get

at it. The kind that has a map pocket on top is best. If you get a magnetic attachment, also add at least one strap, so if the wind blows the bag off, it stays with the bike.

Sleeping bags
It is important to have a bag with the correct temperature rating. Too cold and you will shiver all night. Too warm and you will sweat, which can be dangerous if you get up in freezing weather. Either way, you will not sleep well. I carry two rectangular bags, rated twenty degrees and forty degrees, the forty degree bag is four inches narrower than the other. I can lie on top of both in hot weather. As it gets cooler, I use one as a blanket, then climb in the smaller bag when it gets down around forty degrees, use the larger as a blanket, climb in the larger around twenty degrees, and put the smaller inside the larger if it gets down around zero. The two bags don't weigh ten pounds, and cost seventy dollars. It is important to keep the bags dry. When the are wet or even a little damp, they will not keep you warm. Carry them in a waterproof bag or wrapping, and air them out whenever you can.

Water purifier
Not needed if you will always stay in developed campgrounds, but even then it is a good idea to carry one. Some are very small, even as little as a drinking straw; you just suck the water through it. You will find a variety of them at sporting goods stores. Be aware that a *filter* is different from a *purifier*. A filter will take out microorganisms, but not most minerals; a purifier will get them all. Berkey makes very good purifiers.

Water jugs
Always carry water. You may get stranded for a couple of days, and many campgrounds and camp sites lack water. Any suitable container will do. I use half-gallon fruit juice jugs. I made a pair of saddle bags that hang over the back of the saddle against the

front of the regular saddlebags. Each holds four jugs, so I carry four gallons, 33 pounds, under my thighs. I travel in deserts a lot. If you do not, you can carry less water. The bags are sewn of cotton duck cloth, with two small trucker straps sewn on. The straps pass under the bags to take the weight of the jugs, and are sewn to the bags at the bottom and each top edge. I can adjust the length of the straps to make the jugs ride just on the passenger foot pegs, where they do not touch the pipes or motor.

I also have a cord that ties to one arm of the sissy bar and reaches to the rear of the main saddle and back to the other arm of the sissy bar; a hook on the end clips to the sissy bar. I pass this around the water-bag straps to keep the bags from slipping forward.

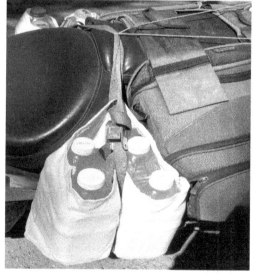

Tent with groundcloth

For short trips and trips where you expect to not need a tent at all, you can get a little one-man bivy (short for bivouac) tent. It is good for keeping mosquitos away and for the unexpected rain, but it is cramped, just large enough for one person to lie down. It is small and light, and fine for sleeping, but just imagine spending all day in it! For longer trips, you want a larger tent. For short trips alone, the smallest you should get is about seven foot square; a two- or three-man tent works. You can make a good back rest of your gear, and spend a rainy day in reasonable comfort. For longer trips, a month or more, get a tent that is large enough to allow you to stand upright. If you get stuck in a two or three day rain, you want to be able to stand erect at times, such as when changing clothes. The smallest tent I have found that is tall enough is a six-man tent. It only cost seventy dollars. The rated sizes are pretty cramped, so I recommend you get a tent rated for at least twice as many people as will be using it. That leaves room for your gear, and enough space to roll over without waking your neighbor. In areas with a lot of flying insects, especially mosquitos and gnats, a larger tent with a screened porch is well worth having. When two or more people are traveling together, only one has to carry the tent. The others can pack some of his gear.

Most tents, even the plastic ones, are not really waterproof. If you touch the inside while it is raining, you compress the fibers, and it will then leak from that spot. So, when you store gear inside, make sure it is not touching the fabric. If the tent seams are taped, they should not leak. For untaped seams, get a bottle of seam sealer and apply per the directions. Dome tents come with a rain fly. Smaller ones are okay for light rain and little wind, but for prolonged heavy rain and stronger winds, you need a full-fly design.

Be aware that the popular plastic tents are not very durable. They break down under UV light. I found they would last about eight months or so before becoming too fragile. They also cannot handle winds much over 35 MPH. They tend to lie down under strong winds, which stresses the fiberglass poles and may break or splinter them. (Splintered poles can be repaired with duck tape.) Strong gusting winds can shred them. The older the tent, the more likely it is to come apart in strong winds.

I finally got fed up with the flimsy things and switched to canvas. The smallest suitable canvas tent I could find weighs 68 pounds, which is too much for a single camper. It cost over $500. A group can manage it, as they can distribute gear and share the load. I ended up making a tent from 10-ounce cotton duck. It weighs about thirty pounds, poles and all, and cost less then three hundred dollars. I expect the tent to last at least ten years, which would take $900 worth of plastic tents to match.

Whatever tent you get, even a bivy, you should use a groundcloth under it. It reduces abrasion of the tent floor, and also helps keep it dry. If water runs under the tent, it will seep through under the pressure of you lying on it, and soak your sleeping bag. Cut your groundcloth one foot smaller that the tent floor and put a grommet in each corner. Tie short loops of rope in each corner so the tent pegs will just fit and will hold the groundcloth centered under the tent. Make very sure that no edge of the groundcloth protrudes from under the tent, otherwise rain running down the side will get between the groundcloth and the tent floor and seep through. Also be sure the top of the groundcloth and the bottom of the tent floor are clean; sand and gravel will abrade the fabric.

Examine the ground where the tent will stand with an eye to water runoff. Some campgrounds have a graveled driveway for RVs. Often this is the best spot to pitch the tent. The gravel is not uncomfortable under a sleeping bag, and generally allows good water runoff. The best site is on a slight rise; the worst is the bottom of a gully. If the land is quite flat, you may need to dig a ditch around the base of the tent to drain water away.

Before pitching the tent, figure out just where you will lie to sleep. If there is any slope to the ground, position your head at the high end. Clear out any rocks or stones, and smooth any hummocks and holes. If you are going to stay there long enough to make it worthwhile, a layer of dry pine needles or leaves, with no twigs included, can add a bit of comfort. Dig a hip hole where your hips will be, about two or three feet wide and an inch deep or less, and pile the dirt where your waist will be. Lie in it to test comfort, and make it deeper or shallower as needed. Check for ridges where your thighs cross the hole and smooth it out. When you get it right, lay the groundcloth and double-check the position, then erect your tent. You may be amazed how comfortable it will be.

Rope
Never travel without rope. A 100 foot climbing rope, 5/8 or 3/4 inch, is a lifesaver. I carry one, which *did* save a life. A biker had gone over a cliff, and was bleeding some forty feet below. His buddies used my rope to reach him and stop the bleeding till help arrived twenty minutes later. The paramedics said he would have bled to death before they got there. Carry a rope.

Also carry fifty feet of 3/8 or 1/4 inch rope (or both), and fifty or a hundred of 1/8 inch. They have a great many uses. When camping out, you should keep any food that animals (squirrels and ravens) can get at in a large bag, and use the 3/8 inch rope to hang the bag from a tree out of their reach. 1/8 inch rope can be used to repair an old saddlebag. I stretched an old set almost two years before I could find a suitable replacement set; they probably had thirty feet of rope holding them together. Carry the rope. You will use it.

Axe, hatchet or machete
Something to cut firewood. I carry a sort of machete: A Special Projects Kukri from Cold Steel. It can cut through a 1 1/2 inch branch with one stroke, and chop an eight inch log faster than a hatchet, but it is not much good for splitting logs. An axe is good for splitting, but not really needed. A good hatchet is more useful. A good machete will do everything a hatchet will do, except serve as a hammer, and a rock will do for that. Whatever you choose, keep it sharp, and be sure you have a good sheath for it, to protect the edge and to prevent accidental cuts.

Shovel
Mostly for digging cat-holes and slit trenches when there is no toilet or outhouse available, and for digging fire pits. I once carried a little one, about four inches by five when folded, patterned on the GI entrenching tool. It was ideal for a backpacker, but with the greater capacity of a bike, I found a full-size GI tool was better. I also carried a full size shovel, because I could, and I spend a lot of time in areas where fire danger is an important consideration. But I found that carrying only the GI tool was good enough. Be sure to get high quality; the cheap ones will bend and break pretty easily.

Pocket knife and sheath knife
You should always carry a good pocket knife. In addition, a spare multi-tool knife such as a Leatherman or Swiss Army Knife should be in your emergency kit. A trained survivor can survive anywhere in America with only a knife; even an untrained person will find he is using a knife more than any other tool. You also must carry a good sheath knife, with at least an eight-inch blade. The sheath knife is more important than the pocket knife. Almost anything you can do with a small knife can be done with a big one, and there is a lot a big one can do that is impossible for a small knife. Stainless steel is good in that it does not rust, but a good high-carbon steel is best, because it will hold an edge better.

The best knife steel is Carbon-V, developed by Cold Steel, and used for several of their knives, but they no longer make it. However, you can still find Carbon-V knives on Ebay. The best knife I have ever used is a Cold Steel Trail Master. I bought one about twenty years ago. I wear it almost all of the time. After the bike, it is my most expensive and valuable piece of equipment.

Always keep your knives sharp. Carry your whetstone in your pocket, and use it to touch up the edge almost every time you use a knife. The pocket knife should have two cutting blades. A razor edge will dull quickly, and usually is not needed. Put a good edge on the larger blade, but not sharp enough to shave the hairs from your arm. Keep a razor edge on the smaller blade for those times when it is needed.

Tarp for the load
If your duffel bags are not waterproof, get a waterproof tarp. Most, such as the cheap woven plastic ones, will shed water, but are not truly waterproof. If it does not have grommets on the edges, add some. Thread a small rope through the grommets, drape the tarp over the load, and tighten the rope so the tarp edges are drawn together under the load and over the saddlebags. Get a tarp no larger than you need, so it doesn't billow and flap in the wind; a 5x7 or 6x8 should do. You can form-fit the cover, but if you leave it as a plain rectangle, you can use it in camp for such things as covering your firewood to keep it dry, or setting a windbreak for your fire.

Grommet kit
You can pick these up at most hardware stores, and packs of more grommets; they are not expensive, and easy to use. You can make sacks with grommets on top to thread draw-strings; it is a lot easier than sewing a drawstring into the hem. Grommets will tear out of tarps and need replacement. I even added grommets to the

tail of a rain jacket to make a waterproof cover for my sleeping bag roll. It works flawlessly, and gives me a spare raincoat.

Straps and caribiner clips
Ropes and bungees have their uses, but for securing a load, I prefer trucker's straps. You don't need expensive heavy-duty ones, cheap 90-pound load straps work fine. Caribiner clips are patterned on the mountain-climbing gear, but not as strong; most have load ratings of only thirty or sixty pounds. They come in various sizes, and have many uses. I have a water bottle hanging from my dashboard, tilted so I can sip without taking my eyes off the road. A little cord with a clip on the end keeps it from falling off, and lets me dismount it in an instant. I use medium ones to attach bags on my load: Tent bag, food bag, laundry bag. About the only thing I use bungees for is to hold the food and laundry bags in place; never for anything heavy.

Map case
A Rand-McNally Road Atlas is all you need for most travel. Get the big one, as it has more detail. Make a waterproof map case big enough to hold the Road Atlas and a lot of fold-up maps. Make it wide enough to let you easily remove and replace the Atlas, and four to six inches taller, so you can fold the top over to keep the rain out. I made mine from a long piece of tarp, and four times as long as the case would be. Folding it over and sewing the sides and bottom gave me a case with three compartments, one for the Atlas and the other two for small maps. I tie the map case to the inside of the windscreen, near the bottom so it does not block vision. Get local maps on location, such as at National Forests and Parks. You can also order Forest and Park maps on the internet, mostly ten dollars each. They show all of the roads and campgrounds, and tell you what facilities (such as water) are at each, and their altitudes and when they are open. There are also park and forest newsletters which list most forest rules and current prices for campgrounds.

The Lonesome Hillbilly

Camp chair
Available at sporting goods stores and Wal-Mart and such. Get the kind that folds into a six inch bundle. It is very light and easy to carry, and makes a big difference in camp comfort. When you are getting one, check it out carefully; some have straight backs, some are more like a recliner. I like the straight ones better. My favorite is the Ozark Trails Oversize model, $15. When you are getting up from one, do not put your hands on the arms and push, because the metal tube can bend. Instead, slide forward so you are sitting on the edge and lean forward. You can put your hands on the edge of the seat and push there, but leaning forward is usually enough.

Toilet paper
Campgrounds almost always provide toilet paper, but they do run out now and then. Dispersed campsites usually have suitable leaves, but they have drawbacks, too. Dried leaves can crumble and leave sharp bits behind. Green leaves work well, but be very careful not to use poison ivy, oak or sumac. Carry the paper in a plastic bag, to keep it dry and to avoid abrading it; it damages very easily. At campgrounds, the hosts will often replace a half-roll with a full one, and leave the half roll lying on top of the paper rack. If I am running low, I will scarf a half roll to replenish my stock. I like to have two half rolls on hand.

Solar shower
This is a black plastic bag, usually five gallon capacity, with a short hose and nozzle, and a rope for hanging. You fill it with water and lay it in the sun till the water is hot enough (and it can get hot enough to scald you). Hang it from a tree branch and take your shower. First use enough water to get yourself wet, then shut it off and do your soaping and scrubbing, then rinse off. It is not luxurious, but it will get you clean. You can get a good one for under ten dollars. The plastic handle is rather weak, and in time, will tear. I used a synthetic fabric pillowcase (because

cotton will rot if left wet) to make a sack to hold the shower bag. A hole at the lower end with hemmed edges lets the outlet cap show through, and a rope handle securely sewn into the open end serves to carry and hang the bag. Thus I never use the plastic handles, so it never tears. I recommend that groups carry one bag per person, so everyone can shower on the same day.

The shower is also excellent for dousing campfires. Instead of just pouring four or five gallons of water over the fire, you can sprinkle where the water is needed, and thoroughly douse the fire with only a gallon or two of water.

Notebooks and pens
I carry a little memo book for shopping lists and such, and a larger book for writing. Since pens are easy to lose, I always carry several. The paper can also be used to start fires.

Camera
You will often see things you want to photograph. You probably have a cell phone with a camera, which is fine for snapshots. I like to carry a larger digital camera, too. Take *lots* of pictures. They cost nothing.

Binoculars
A small pair of roof-prism design, about 8x21 power, is about the size of a deck of cards. It is not as good as a full size set, but unless you are doing serious bird-watching or star-gazing, it is quite good enough, and maybe a twentieth the size and weight.

Canteen for hiking and riding
Mostly I carry water in half-gallon juice jugs, but also a bottle for hiking and to sip from when riding. A quart canteen is great for hiking. The kind with a felt pouch or lining will keep water cooler if made wet. But I have an insulated bottle with a sip spout which I attach to my dashboard, where I can sip from it without

taking my eyes off the road, and can also hang from my belt for hiking. A Camel-Back pack is also a good choice.

Radio
Solar or, preferably, crank charged, with a weather channel. It is very useful for planning your next move to another camp, and for day-to-day activities. The weather channel picks up local weather data, each station covering a small area, usually about a fifty mile circle. There are many on the market, but most of them are trash. The best I have found is the Eton Scorpion II. It is about five inches by two by one and a half, with solar and crank charging, rubber shock protection, and a clip loop on one end. It also includes a clock and a flashlight, picks up AM and FM, and has two USB outlets for charging small devices such as cell phones. I have known it to pick up transmissions when no one else's radios could. It cost fifty dollars, about twice what the others did, but it works, and they don't.

Sunscreen
I never use it myself, but it is a good idea if you have light skin, no tan, and you are going to desert or high elevation, but it blocks vitamin D production. I consider the "degrading ozone layer" to be superstition. UV is good for your health, as long as you don't get too much.

Emergency Kit   (See the Emergency Kit chapter.)

Tool Kit

Where you carry the tools is a very important factor. You can make a pair of bags similar to the water bags, and hang them behind the saddle bags. One carries your tool kit and other heavy stuff, the other (well away from the pipes!) carries your gas can.

Or, if you have pipes on both sides, the second bag can hold heavy food, such as rice and flour, while the gas can rides higher.

Stow the tool kit, or at least the ones for bike repairs, where you can get at it easily, because if you need it, you do not want to have to unload the bike to get at it. Also, you should carry it with the bike at all times. Unload your camping gear, but when you make short trips, sightseeing or going to town for food or to do laundry, carry the repair kit and other bike tools with you. I learned that lesson the hard way.

Standard bike tools for your model bike.
Usually, the little tool kit that comes with the bike is enough. Add whatever tools you like, such as an oil filter wrench and a torque wrench, but only what you need.

Puncture repair kit and air pump
For tubeless tires, get a common kit that includes rubber cement, rubber plugs, and the tools to prepare the hole and insert the plugs. For tubes, get a liquid sealer such as Slime or a similar product. You can carry a manual pump, or an electric one that runs off your battery.

If you use a Slime-type sealer, make sure it is designed for motorcycles; the car type will corrode aluminum wheels. I would not use sealers except in tubes, because mechanics hate the stuff; they will probably charge you extra for the clean-up required, or refuse to change the tire. I suppose it is okay in a tube, if you replace the tube instead of patch it. If you do an emergency puncture repair, have a permanent plug put in soon; the temporary plugs are only good for maybe a hundred miles or so.

Duck tape
(The original tape was made of cotton duck with adhesive added, so it was called "duck tape". Later it was used for air ducts, and

became called "duct tape". That is the legend, and I find it amusing, so I call it duck tape.) Great stuff for emergency repairs. Get cheap brand made with rubber adhesive. Use it for emergency repairs such as patching rips in clothes till you have time to do a proper repair, and for holding wounds closed. It has many other uses, including a fire starter. Tear off a foot or two and wad it very loosely. Place it under your tinder and kindling and light it. It will burn even when wet, and burns long and hot. (This is why you get the rubber cement kind; rubber cement is what Hollywood uses to make spectacular fires. Gorilla Tape is excellent for holding things together, but it does not burn. Whatever kind you get, test it and make sure it will burn well.)

Baling wire
Also good for repairs, especially where duck tape won't work, such as on the muffler pipes. The wire used for binding rebar at construction sites is basically the same thing.

WD-40
Good for freeing stuck parts and for drying electronics. It is not a good lubricant, so after freeing parts, oil them.

There is an old joke about the Redneck Repair Kit: Duck Tape and WD-40. "If it's movin' an' shouldn't, use duck tape; if it ain't movin' an' should, use WD-40". There is a lot of truth in that joke.

3-in-1 oil
Good all purpose lubricant, especially to clean up after using WD-40.

Knife sharpener
A dull knife is dangerous; You put a lot of pressure on the knife, so if it slips, you can easily cut yourself very badly. Get a small stone of whatever kind you prefer, and learn to use it properly.

There are many expert opinions, often contradictory. Learn a way that works for you; it is not hard. My preference is a diamond hone, a steel plate with tiny diamond chips embedded in the surface. It is light weight and works on large and small knives. I have been using mine for some twenty years, and it still works as new. There are also sharpeners designed for kitchen knives. The good ones work well and quickly, but they do not give you an edge as sharp or long-lasting as you can get with a whetstone. Use one if you wish, or if you don't know how to use a stone.

Spare fuses (at least three of each size)
Spare light bulbs (at least one of each size your bike uses)
Spare control cables and tubes
A broken clutch cable can strand you. I have spare cables and brake fluid tubes installed next to the ones that are connected. If one fails, all I have to do is hook up the spare, and maybe add brake fluid, and I am moving again.

Shorty hammer
If you do not carry a hatchet, a hammer is convenient for driving tent pegs. A rock will do the job, so you don't really *have* to carry a hammer. I carry a shorty in my tent bag.

Diagonal cutters, for the baling wire

Boiled Linseed Oil
Neatsfoot Oil
These are vital for caring for wood and leather gear. I mention them here because you will need them, but treatment is not needed often, so you won't need to pack them with you. I live on the road, so I pack them. Also, boiled linseed oil and mineral spirits mixed 50/50 are the best waterproofing I have found for canvas tents. Not so good for duffel bags, because it doesn't make the cloth actually water *proof*, just very water *repellent*.

Cooking Kit

Camp stove
A camp stove is far more convenient than building a campfire, and does not dirty your pans with soot. If you are going to have a fire anyway, cook over it if you wish. But there will be times when you cannot have a campfire, so you either use a camp stove or eat sandwiches and canned goods. Propane or butane stoves are common, the small ones are pretty cheap, and fuel cylinders are readily available. I carry a Coleman Sportster II Dual Fuel stove, which you can get from Amazon for about sixty dollars. It burns either white gas or unleaded gasoline. Unleaded gas is less than a quarter the cost of propane cylinders or white gas, you can get it at any gas station, and you don't have to carry fuel for the stove because you already have a gas can for the bike. It is easy to use, and does *not* make food taste of gasoline. One part, called the generator, will clog up in time and may need replacement, so I always carry a spare.

Big pot with lid
The big pot is used for soups and stews, for boiling water for pasta, for disinfecting water, and for a sink when you are washing up. It need not be of heavy gauge metal; the cheap thin ones do just fine. The minimum size should be two inches wider than your small pot and about twice as deep. When packed, your smaller pot and most of your other cooking gear fits inside the big pot.

Small pot with lid
Stanley makes an excellent camp kit. It includes a one quart pot with a lid and a handle, two plastic bowls with lids, and a collapsible ladle and spatula, which all nest inside the pot. The lid has several vent holes which I had to plug up with high-temperature plastic, otherwise I couldn't cook rice in it. Even so, I strongly recommend it.

Cast iron frying pan, 8"
Cast iron frying pan, 10" with lid
Nothing cooks as well as cast iron, especially over a campfire, which is very irregular heat. The ten-inch pan is needed for frying onions and potatos and steaks and such. I used to carry a ten-inch dutch oven, but cooking for just one or two people, the large fry pan with the dutch oven lid is big enough and works just fine. I also carry an eight inch pan because it is just right for cooking eggs and pancakes and for baking bannock bread. I could do without the small one, but I like it.

Meat thermometer
Needed because campfire heat is irregular. Instant read is best.

Long spoon, fork, ladle and spatula
Useful for cooking over a fire to avoid getting scorched. However, wearing a long-sleeve denim shirt and heavy leather gloves will protect you just as well, so short utensils will do.

Cutting board, 7"x9"
Not really necessary, but very useful when you need a clean and flat surface for preparing food. Wood or plastic, as you prefer.

Bowl
Something to eat from; you only need one per person. The Stanley kit I described above has two good bowls, big enough for most meals, but not for spaghetti or noodles or such. That is okay, you can always have seconds.

Fork and spoon
A *real* fork and spoon, not these fancy pocket knives with fork and spoon blades. Not a spork, either. They hardly weigh anything, so go with the comfort. Carry a spare, too. Your meals will be more enjoyable.

Salt, pepper and spices
Salt is vital in the wild, especially the desert and high dry altitudes. Pepper and spices are luxuries, but their tiny weight set against the great difference they make in food make them more than worthwhile. Pick your own favorites.

Jars for oils
I carry two quart-size mayonaisse jars, one for bacon grease, one for clarified butter. I also have an eight-ounce Gator-Ade bottle for olive oil, because olive oil bottles do not seal well. Any jars or bottles you carry must be leakproof, Plastic is better than glass, as it is lighter and doesn't break.

Paper towels
These are extremely handy to have around. I look for a brand that has the perforations very close together, around five inches. I then slice the roll in half with a very sharp knife and store each half in a plastic bag. This gives you very small towels, which is ample most of the time, and you can always tear off two or three if you need a larger one. You could use a washcloth instead, but you would have to wash and dry it frequently.

Dish soap
A very small bottle. You do not need much, and can buy more.

Body soap
Get a clean bio-degradable bar, such as castile soap or coal tar soap or Ivory Soap, not the modern scented stuff such as Dial or Zest. Carry it in a plastic bag.

Scrubber
The green coarse plastic pads work well.

Bags for big pot and frying pans
These are tough waterproof bags, one for the big pot, one for the

frying pans. If you don't get *all* of the soot and grease off of the pots, it can ruin your other stuff. These bags will keep it safe.

Dutch oven
Really a necessity for campfire cooking. Carry one big enough to feed everyone in your party. As I mentioned above, a ten-inch frying pan with a lid is a good dutch oven for two.

Grill
I also carry an eighteen inch wire grill. It is very handy when cooking over a rock-ring fire, weighs almost nothing, and when packed upright by my sissy bar, takes up no space. If you carry one, also carry a small wire brush for cleaning it.

Coffee pot
Last in the list because I don't drink coffee, so it was a last-minute addition. You can get a plain pot to heat water, or a percolator type with an insert for grounds.

Clothes Kit

Boots
Forget the engineer's boots or biker boots; the engineer's boots are not good for hiking, and neither are most biker boots. Get good hiking boots, at least ankle high, and break them in well before you leave. If the boots are suede, keep them treated with a good oil. If they are smooth, keep them polished with a paste polish, not liquid. This keeps the boots water resistant.

Shoes
You also should have a pair of canvas shoes such as sneakers or deck shoes, for wearing around camp. You need to let boots and shoes dry and air out frequently, so never go on a trip with just your boots.

Sandals
Flip-flops or some other kind of sandals are useful for getting up in the middle of the night and for going swimming.

Long pants, 3
Tough long pants are vital when hiking through brush and cactus. Denim is best, except in cold and wet, when wool is better. To save space, I have woolen long underwear, and wear denim over them. Wool is comfortable even when wet; cotton is not. You can wear your pants and shirts a week or so if you don't sweat a lot. Three sets lets you do laundry every two weeks or so.

Short pants
Sometimes short pants are more comfortable. They also double as a bathing suit, and as something to wear in a camp shower.

Long sleeve shirt, 2
Like long pants, you need long sleeves in brush or cactus country. They also serve as another layer in cold weather, and as sun protection.

T-shirts, 4
I wear them alone or under a long-sleeve shirt. Three or four days is about the limit for wearing one between washings.

Underpants, 4
Socks, 4
You should wash your feet and groin every day, and change your underpants and socks. They can easily be rinsed out, so you don't actually need fifteen pairs to last between bi-weekly washings.

Bandanna, 3
Big ones, like eighteen inches square. Good for handkerchiefs, wet headgear to keep cool, or worn bandit-style to keep out dust, and many other uses.

Belt
One is enough, of strong webbing or leather. If you have a big belly, suspenders work better and are more comfortable.

Towel
You must always know where your towel is.

Rain gear (jacket, pants, boot covers, gloves)
Pack these where they are readily available. Mountain weather can change rapidly, and you may need to get them out quickly. Riding in the rain is not bad if you slow down and stay alert; if you are wet and cold, your attention is on being uncomfortable and on getting to your destination, not your riding. If your bike jacket and boots are waterproof, you need only pants and gloves.

Helmet with visor
There is a freedom to riding without a helmet, but there are also hazards; I once rode through a swarm of bees, and if I had not been wearing a helmet and visor, I would have had a dozen or two frightened bees in my hair and beard. I also wear glasses, so I need a visor at higher speeds to keep them from blowing off; usually I ride with the visor up. My compromise is to use a half-helmet, as that is the smallest I have found that has three-snap fasteners, and cheap replaceable three-snap visors. Clear ones, not tinted. Tinted visors are fine during the day, but dangerous at night. In some places, they are even illegal at night. Changing visors is a big hassle, and sunglasses work just as well.

Helmet liner
Something to cover your ears and neck in cold weather. Even in August, riding at 11,000 feet can be bitter.

Sunglasses
I almost never use them; they are rarely necessary, such as in a snow-field with blinding glare. Sometimes, when riding into the

sunrise or sunset, the glare will make it hard to see. That is almost the only time you need sunglasses.

Riding gloves
Work gloves
I do not know anyone who disdains riding gloves. I have a pair of medium-thick leather for most riding, and a pair of waterproof insulated gloves for riding in rain and cold. Never use riding gloves for anything except riding, or keeping hands warm in camp. For work and cooking, use leather gloves from the hardware store. They are a lot cheaper, and actually better suited for work.

Chaps
Good stout leather chaps protect your shins from highway pebbles and wind chill. They are also good enough protection from light rain.

Kidney belt
For many people, a kidney belt is a must for long rides. I do not use them, but if you are prone to lower back pain, get one.

Hat, wide brim
Cowboy hat. Stetson. Sombrero. It helps keep your head cool, and your eyes and ears and neck shaded. This can be very important in the Wilds, especially in the desert, where it helps protect you from sunstroke. Wool felt will deform when it gets wet, and over time lose its shape and become just a felt sack. Fur felt is much more expensive, but will last for years. Canvas or heavy fabric is also good, but make sure it does not have a cardboard core. Straw hats can be good, but will not last long. I once had a plastic straw hat from a 99-cent store. It wore out in less than two years, but was quite satisfactory while it lasted. Get a hat with a long chin strap; you will need it in wind, and it will allow you to hang your hat behind your neck when riding. That is

usually the best place to carry the hat on the road; it will not get crushed, and it is right there when you dismount.

Bag for dirty clothes
Obviously, you want to keep clean and dirty clothes separate. A large enough lightweight bag is a great place to store them. It is carried on top of everything else (where it gets aired), and when it is time to hit the laundromat, you just grab the bag.

Laundry soap
I carry a small bag of laundry soap, rather than buy it at each laundromat. It is a lot cheaper, and not inconvenient, because I carry it in my laundry bag. It is also a good idea to hang on to quarters, enough to do at least one batch of laundry. Often the laundromat will have no detergent or coin changer available.

Sewing Kit

Needles, various sizes
A few needles, three or four, small medium and large, plus a curved needle, are all you need. You probably will not be making anything, just doing repairs. Do the repairs as soon as possible, because rips will get larger and be harder to fix. I live on the road, so I carry a few special needles, because I sometimes *do* make things, mostly sacks such as my water saddlebags, but I also built a complete 8x10 tent.

Fine thread
Heavy thread
Cotton, wool, synthetic, it doesn't much matter. Fine thread for when strength is not an issue (t-shirts and such), heavy thread for jeans and jackets. Actually, I no longer carry fine thread. Color is purely esthetic. I carry white and black. Suit yourself.

Stitch-awl with waxed thread
Now, this one is almost vital. The Stewart Stitch-All is the best, but the Tandy Leather model is also very good. It has a spool of heavy waxed thread inside a largish round handle and a heavy needle with the eye in the point. You can easily drive it through leather or several layers of denim or other heavy cloth, and lay in a lock-stitch quickly. It comes with a second needle with a slightly curved tip, for times you can only work from one side of the material. You can buy replacement spools of thread, or a 270 yard roll, at most leather supply stores. I never travel without it.

Safety pins, various sizes
From half inch to two inch, they are excellent for a quick fix. I carry my emergency kit in a fisherman's vest, and use small safety pins to keep inner pockets closed. Nothing can fall out, and I have a few more pins for emergency use. When sewing, I use them instead of straight pins. Anything a straight pin can do, a safety pin can, too, so don't bother with carrying straight pins. Unless you want to.

Scissors
Besides cutting cloth and trimming patches, they also open tough bags and trim hair. A good small set with a four inch blade will do nicely. But get a good set, not a cheap one.

Measuring tape
The cloth or plastic sewing tape, not the steel construction worker's tool. The steel one will do, but for our purposes, the cloth one is better. It is lighter and more compact, and it doesn't really get used that much. But when you need it, it can prevent wasteful errors.

First Aid Kit

Band-aids

Get a box of assorted sizes; the brand does not matter. When you get a cut or a scrape, *use* them. In the Wild, an infected cut can be life-threatening, especially if you are alone, and they are easy to infect. There is much more life out here, especially microscopic, than you will find in the cities and towns. And if you are a thousand miles from home, there may be germs you have never been exposed to. Treat cuts and scrapes immediately. If you have clean water, water which you could drink, wash out the wound. *Never* use lake or pond water that you would not drink to wash a wound; better to not wash it. Clean it as well as you can, then treat it with tincture of iodine. It stings, but it is worth it. If you are in conditions where the wound will get dirty, cover the wound with a bandage to keep dirt out and prevent re-infection. Change the bandage daily till the wound closes and scabs over. The wound will heal best and fastest if it is exposed to clean air, but sometimes you have to protect it.

Large sterile gauze pads
Adhesive tape

For wounds that are too big for a band-aid, use gauze pads and adhesive tape to make a large enough cover.

Ace bandages, ankle and rib sizes

The only treatment for cracked ribs is a tight wrapping and minimal motion. And a sprained ankle will heal faster and let you get around a bit if you keep it tightly wrapped. Ace bandages are ideal for this. Be sure to get good expensive ones with steel clips. The cheap ones with aluminum clips don't last long, and the clips often will fail on the first use, much less be reusable. You will need to rewrap a sprained ankle daily, to wash and massage it; your bandage clips must be reusable.

Iodine
Not mercurochrome or "deodorized" iodine; get the pure, plain stuff, a 2% iodine solution. It may be hard to find, but Walgreen's carries it. Besides using it to disinfect cuts, you can disinfect water for drinking. For clear water, add six drops per quart, mix it well, and leak a little over the opening of the container to disinfect the opening. Let it sit for fifteen minutes. For cloudy water, strain it through a fine cloth such as a T-shirt, then add twelve drops per quart, and let it sit for one hour. Boiling the water for ten minutes is better, if you can do it. A small eye-dropper is good to carry, especially if you will be disinfecting water frequently.

Cotton swabs
All-around useful. There is a lot of dirt and dust out here, and cotton swabs can clean it out of most small places. They are good for cleaning wounds and ears, too.

Emergency Kit

Hopefully you will never need it, but if you ever do, this may save your life. It is a small collection of tools and supplies, little things most people normally never think of, vital if you get lost or stranded, but sometimes useful in normal circumstances. Even thou there are many items in it, it is small enough to carry *all* of the time, and not be inconvenient. Get good quality materials, because they are not that expensive, and your life may depend on them. I have never actually needed mine (possibly because I always have it), but I know several people who maintain they are only alive because they had a kit when they needed it.

Container
This can be anything convenient: A fisherman's vest, a fanny pack, a web belt with many clip-on pockets. It should hold

everything and be comfortable enough to wear all of the time, even (in emergencies) while you sleep. If you don't have it with you, it does no good. I use a vest with many pockets for the smaller items, and a fanny pack for the bulky stuff.

Knife

You should always carry a good pocket knife. In addition, a spare multi-tool knife such as the Leatherman should be in your emergency kit. A trained survivor can survive anywhere in America with only a knife; even an untrained person will find he is using a knife more than any other tool.

Whetstone

A dull knife is dangerous. You put a lot of pressure on the knife, so if it slips, you can easily cut yourself very badly. Get a small stone of whatever kind you prefer, and learn to use it properly. There are many expert opinions, often contradictory. Learn a way that works for you; it is not hard. My preference is a diamond hone, a steel plate with tiny diamond chips embedded in the surface. It is light weight and works on large and small knives. I have been using mine for some twenty years, and it still works as new.

Matches

This is the most important item in the kit after a knife. Get large waterproof and windproof matches. Also get a metal or plastic container to carry them. If they are not strike-anywhere, carry a striking surface in the container, and a spare in a waterproof container elsewhere in the kit. Some brands are good matches, but the box they are in is not waterproof, and the striking surface does not work when it is wet. You can waterproof stick matches by dipping them in wax or nail polish, but the commercial wind-proof ones are much better. The better ones are so effective, you can't even blow them out intentionally.

Butane Lighters
The cheap disposables are good enough most of the time. They do not work when the flint gets wet or when it is very cold. Use them when you can, and save the matches for when you really need them. I always carry several.

Fire Striker
A rod of flammable metal with a striker. You shave off a little metal to use as tinder, then use the striker to make a spark. They work under all conditions, but are nowhere near as easy to use as matches. This is the last-ditch *emergency* emergency fire starter.

Three ways of making fire? Yes. It is that important.

Candle
For lighting fires under bad conditions. The candle burns longer than a match, and is more wind-proof and waterproof. Little tea candles an inch diameter and quarter inch thick are best. Place one under your twigs and light it. It will usually light even damp twigs.

First Aid Kit
This is a second kit. You have the one you normally use, plus this very small one for the emergency kit. It can be a small commercial kit, or you can assemble your own. It should be in a waterproof container, and contain just the basics: Band-Aids, sterile gauze, adhesive tape, a four inch Ace bandage with steel (not weak aluminum) clasps, and any special medicine you need. Mine, aside from the Ace bandage, fills an Altoids tin, and is sealed with duck tape.

Tincture of Iodine
Not mercurochrome or "deodorized" iodine; get the pure, plain stuff, a 2% iodine solution. Besides using it to disinfect cuts,, you can disinfect water for drinking. For clear water, add six drops

per quart, mix it well, and leak a little over the opening of the container to disinfect the opening. Let it sit for fifteen minutes. For cloudy water, strain it through a fine cloth such as a T-shirt, then add twelve drops per quart, and let it sit for one hour. Boiling the water for ten minutes is better, if you can do it.

Plastic Bag
A one-gallon heavy-duty freezer bag with a zip lock seal is best. Use it for disinfecting water, two or three quarts at a time.

Paracord
Fifty feet of genuine 550 paracord is useful for many things, especially in survival situations: Snares, tourniquets, quick repairs, bundling small things like fish or animals caught in snares, tying your emergency blanket to a tree for a sunshade or rain shelter, tying cloth or bark or leaves to make a hat or cloak. You get the idea. There are many cheap imitations, so be sure to get the real thing: It comprises a woven sheath enclosing eleven strands of fifty-pound test cords, so it has a rated breaking strength of 550 pounds. You can take it apart to use the smaller strands as string or fishing line or whatever. Some people use it for shoelaces so they always have it handy. One woman I know braided a belt from it. Clever!

Cell Phone
Some would rank this higher because it is such an easy way to get help. I place it down this far because it can fail (get wet, run out of power, be in a non-reception area), and if it does, and you depend on it, you may be dead. You can use it to call for help, but did you know it can be used to track you? If you call 911 from the middle of the woods, the police can read your exact location and send help right to you. (If you don't want to be tracked, turn the phone off and pull the battery.) Always carry your phone. It would be smart to carry a quick-charger, too.

Fishing Kit
Hooks, small, medium and large, four to eight of each. Several sizes of lead sinkers, at least a dozen. Two 25 foot lengths of monofilament line, 40 pound test. Six swivels. Mine all fits into an Altoids Smalls tin.

Sewing Kit
Light and heavy thread; wind it on a piece of cardboard so you don't carry the bulky spool. At least six needles of small and large sizes. At least a dozen safety pins, small and large. You do not need straight pins; safety pins will do the job. This also fits in an Altoids Smalls tin.

Flashlight
LED type with a crank generator so you do not need batteries, with a clip or loop so you can tie it to your vest or belt. Get a good one; Eveready makes one for about twelve dollars.

Pepper Spray
(If you are going to bear country.) Get one that is easy for you to operate, 10% strength, that you can carry where you can get at it quickly. Get two, then use one up practicing with it. Know how far it will reach, and how it behaves in wind. Wash your hands after using it, and be careful using it, so you do not get it in your eyes.

Stun gun
High-voltage zapper. They are proving to be an even better bear-deterrent than pepper spray. If a bear is threatening, zap repeatedly, two or three times per second. You do not need to touch the bear with it. Apparently the sound is painful, and the ozone smell seems to scare them, like lightning. Forest rangers are carrying them in bear country. So why carry this *and* pepper spray? Because the zapper may run out of charge.

Pencil
Cut a pencil to about three inches long, and give it a blunt point, about 45 degrees.

Memo Book
2"x4" or smaller. Use it to leave messages and to light fires.

Duck Tape
Get the kind with rubber adhesive, not the brand "Duck Tape" or Gorilla Tape. Use it for emergency repairs such as patching rips in clothes till you have time to do a proper repair, and for holding wounds closed. It has many other uses, including a fire starter. Tear off a foot or two and wad it very loosely. Place it under your tinder and kindling and light it. It will burn even when wet, and burns long and hot. You do not need to carry the whole roll. Carefully wrap it around your pencil, with one edge half way up the metal eraser holder, till it is at least 1/2 inch thick. Make it as thick as you can and still comfortably use the pencil. It is not a bad idea to carry several such rolls, because there are so many things you will find to use it for.

Compass
Any type will do, as long as it is durable and accurate.

Wire Saw
For cutting logs and branches too big for your knife. The cheap ones break easily, so get a good one. You can hold on to the loops if you are only making one or two small cuts, but a six inch stick one inch or so thick can be slipped into each loop to make a comfortable grip you can use for an hour.

Tweezers
Splinters can get infected and cripple you. Get good tweezers whose tips meet closely, so you can grip a tiny splinter. You may need to file them for a perfect fit.

Signal Mirror
Get a real signal mirror, not just a small mirror, made of steel, not glass or plastic. It must be reflective on both the front and back and have a hole in the center. You hold the mirror in one hand, and hold the other hand where the light shining through the hole strikes the hand. Look through the center hole at your target. Tilt the mirror so you can see the other hand reflected in the back of the mirror. Line up the spot of light on your hand with the hole in the mirror. The mirror is then reflecting the sunlight straight at what you see through the hole.

Whistle
Get one that is loud and shrill so it will be heard and noticed a long way off.

Brass Wire
Better than string for making snares and lashing a spear head (such as a knife) to a haft. Do not carry the whole spool, just a dozen or so yards in a small coil.

Mosquito Net
Fits over a wide-brimmed hat to cover the face and neck. Pants, long-sleeve shirt and gloves cover the rest of the body.

Emergency Blanket
Also called space blanket, it is a reflective mylar sheet at least four feet by eight. It can be used to reflect light away to keep you cool in the desert sun, or wrapped around you to insulate and to reflect body heat back in freezing air. Get one that is silver on one side and bright orange on the other for excellent visibility against all backgrounds. They are rather flimsy, so they are no good for everyday use.

GI Can Opener

Very simple and easy to use, it is just two pieces of metal that fold together about one inch by a half inch. It makes a good fishing lure and emergency knife. It can also be used to open tin cans.

Tobacco

If you smoke, add a pack or two of cigarettes or tobacco to your emergency kit, but use them sparingly so they will last. If you are craving a smoke, you will be less alert, and that can kill you. Also, a very effective insect repellent can be made by soaking a little tobacco in water till the water turns brown, then smearing the water on your skin. They are effective for removing ticks: place the glowing tip very close to the tick, and it will let go.

Deck of Cards

Morale is vital to survival, and often neglected. If you can't or shouldn't travel, such as during the day in the desert in summer, you can get bored and restless. Card games can keep you interested and alert. Besides, if you are lost, just start playing solitaire. Someone is sure to come along and tell you to place the red jack on the black queen.

That is the basic list. It is small and compact. There are additional tools that should be carried among your regular gear, but would make your emergency kit too bulky.

Stowage

How you pack your gear is of vital importance; improper packing can cause a wreck. My list may seem like a lot of gear, and it is, but not for camping all year. It weighs less than 150 pounds, and when properly stowed, it is both safe and comfortable.

1. Your bike has a designed load capacity. The load is everything not the bike: You, perhaps a passenger, and all of your gear. Do not exceed the load capacity.
2. Keep the center of gravity as low as possible. Pack the heaviest stuff at the bottom, in the saddlebags. Place the lightest stuff on top. Remember that when the bike is on the kickstand, the load is not centered; too high a center of gravity will topple the bike.
3. Balance the load. Keep the center of gravity in line with the middle of the bike. Balance at each level is good, but not vital; overall balance is what matters. Having the heaviest stuff balanced at the lowest level, then the medium at the next level, and so on, will give you a lower center of gravity. Keep in mind the moment arms, the distance from the center of the bike. Twenty pounds one foot left of center and ten pounds two feet right of center will balance, even when you are banking on a turn. But packing the same thirty pounds, half on each side at equal distances from center provides no advantage as far as stability of the bike is concerned, even when at rest on the kickstand.
4. Strap the load in place firmly so that nothing can shift. A sudden shift can make you drop the bike.

You may have noticed that tires wear more on the left side; the left side is worn out, but the right side is good for another two or three thousand miles. This is because most roads have a camber; they are higher in the center than on the edges. This is done to allow rain to run off. But it also means your tire is pressing harder on the left side, the uphill side, so it wears faster. There are other opinions of why the left side wears faster, but all that matters is the fact that they do. If you can even out the wear, you will extend the life of the tires ten percent or more. There are several tricks to accomplish this. Whenever it is possible and safe, ride on the left side of the road. Then you get the greater wear on the right side of the tread. When you can't ride to the left, stay as close to the center as is safe. When riding in a town, turning right three times instead of turning left once will wear the right side instead of the left. If the town has traffic lights, it is often faster, too. You can also scoot your butt to the left to change the center of gravity. Note, the object is not to increase wear on the right side, but to *shift* wear from the left side to the right side.

The most effective trick lies in stowing your gear. When you load the bike, the common rule is to keep the center of gravity as close to centerline as possible, but if you shift it just a bit to the left, the bike will balance while leaning slightly to the right. That shifts the tread wear to the right. You do not need much; perfection would be matching the angle of the road surface, and you can see how small that angle is. Having the bike leaning slightly does change the way the bike responds; it will have a slight tendency to veer right, so take it easy for a few hundred miles till you learn to deal with it.

Do not rely on bungee cords. If they are not tightly stretched, the load will be a bit loose and can shift. If they are stretched tightly, they will lose strength and may break. Rope is good. Manila and hemp are good, but will rot if left damp. Dacron is better. Nylon is okay, but it will stretch. Polypropylene is slick and may not hold a knot. All synthetics will break down under direct sunlight; they have to be replaced frequently, especially under desert sun. Truckers straps are best. You don't need expensive heavy-duty ones, cheap 90-pound load straps work fine. The straps will deteriorate and wear, so inspect them frequently and replace them as needed. I have secured ropes around my saddlebags, with loops to attach the end hooks on straps. My cargo is packed in a large duffel bag, and the straps go around the duffel and hold it firmly in place. A second duffel bag can be placed on top of the first and strapped to it. I also have a sissy bar, which is ideal for holding the bags in place, so there is no chance of them slipping off the back. It also provides a point to secure another bag or folding chair or whatever behind the sissy bar. This also ensures that most of the load will be forward of the rear wheel hub; too much weight *behind* the wheel will tend to lift the front wheel and reduce your steering ability.

In front of the windshield just above the headlamp is another storage location. Don't put more than ten or fifteen pounds there, or it may interfere with steering. Make sure it does not obscure the headlamp or the turn signals. It's an ideal place for your sleeping bag or tent, maybe both. Besides balancing the weight, you also need to balance the surface area so the wind affects both sides equally, and make it as aerodynamic as you can. And, of course, make sure it does not block your view, and that it cannot fall back and strike you if it comes loose. Likewise, when you pack the gear behind you, make sure it does not block your view in the mirrors. Long brackets that position the mirrors high and wide will give you a better view.

Pack everything in large bags so you have as few items to secure as possible. Make sure each bag is tied to the bike, so that if it does fall off, it will stay with the bike. Try to secure it so it does not actually fall off, but if it does, it cannot get caught in the wheels or chain or belt, and does not interfere with steering.

Never tie anything to any control cable or tube. Never stow or attach anything on the shock absorbers.

A tank bag can be very handy. Get a fairly large one, with a transparent pocket on top to hold a map. It is not vital, but can save you from wrong turns. Magnetic attachment is good, and convenient when gassing up, but also have at least one strap to tie it to the bike, so if it should fall or blow off, it won't land in the road and make you turn back to get it. It is the best place to carry rain gear so you can get at it *fast*. Considering how quickly a rain storm can come up in the mountains, this is important.

When you start off, check the load after a mile or so to make sure everything is secure. Check the load every time you stop, and if you ever suspect something may be loose or have shifted, stop at once to check and correct it. When you have first loaded the bike, practice for the first couple of hundred miles to get the feel for it and adjust your reflexes. Gas mileage will also be lower. The weight and balance will be very different from what you are used to; you will have to corner more slowly because of the greater momentum of the load. At very slow speeds and especially when stopping and starting, it will be harder to control the weight; you can easily drop the bike by leaning just a bit too far. Watch your footing carefully when stopping. I once set my foot on what looked like a smooth grassy area, but actually was an eight inch deep ditch filled with grass right where I stepped. The bike went over, and I had to unpack everything before I could right it.

- Keep your gas can well away from the motor and exhaust pipes. Carry it in a place where you can get at it without having to unload everything.
- Keep meltables (plastics) and flammables away from the motor and exhaust pipes.
- Spend some time figuring the best way to strap or tie the load on. You want the ties secure, durable and simple, and easy and quick to secure and to take off. Straps with clamps are usually best. Custom fit the straps so there is a bit of extra length, but not so much as to leave a length

The Lonesome Hillbilly

hanging that may catch in something or look amateurish.
- Make sure the load does not block your vision in the rear-view mirrors.
- Get or make the largest saddlebags you can; they are the best place to carry heavy gear because they ride so low, so the bigger they are, the better. The largest I have found are made by Chase Harper. 50-caliber ammo cans are very good, except that they open from the top so you have to unload to open them; not a good place for your gas can.
- A tank bag is good for things you want to access quickly. The kind with a clear plastic pocket on top lets you carry a map where you can see it while riding.
- Big heavy-duty canvas duffel bags are my favorite for general stowage. They fit across the passenger seat with the ends on the saddlebags. Get the kind with no compartments inside, and a full-length zipper on the side. Pack your gear in smaller sacks, of different colors or with prominent labels so you quickly find the one you want. Pack the sacks in the duffel bags.
- In your bottom duffel bag, pack a sack of soft things such as clothes in the front center, where it will contact the small of your back. It makes a great backrest to lean on. Hard and pointy items here will be *very* uncomfortable.
- Make two sacks that will each hold two, three or four half-gallon juice jars, the rectangular shape. Attach straps to hang them over the saddle, snug against the front of the saddlebags. That is where you carry your water, as low as you can. I hang mine where they can rest on the passenger foot pegs. I also made a pair of sacks that hang on the rear sides of the saddlebags, where I carry my gas can in one and flour, cornmeal, etc., in the other. In effect, these are extensions of the saddlebags, for carrying heavy stuff low.
- Take care that nothing obscures the taillight or turn signals.

Water

Always carry plenty of water, most especially in very low humidity, high altitudes and arid areas. The usually one gallon per person per day is recommended, twice that in deserts and high temperatures. Drink plenty; you are already dehydrated when you feel thirsty. You can use the trick of carrying a button or a small pebble in your mouth to keep the saliva flowing, but this only eases the symptoms of thirst; it is *not* a substitute for drinking. When you are short on water, do not smoke or drink alcohol or spit; these all waste water. Do not use carbonated sodas or beer unless there is no other choice, and do not carry them in place of water. Do not drink urine. Sure, there are lots of You-Tube videos explaining how to do it and why it is good. They only show that you can drink urine, not that you will survive longer. Your body urinates to get rid of poisons. If you drink urine, your body has to work harder to filter those poisons out again, and ends up using more water than you get from the urine. Do not drink sea-water or salty water or blood, either. Wetting your clothes with salt water or urine will cool you and decrease sweating, but do not drink them.

Water from free-running brooks and streams is usually quite safe. When water filters through sand, many impurities are removed. Even sea-water can be made potable by filtering it through sand. On a seashore or beach, you can dig a hole a few feet from the water's edge and drink the water that seeps in. It may be a bit brackish, but it is drinkable. Water from stagnant pools is not safe. Puddles that have just formed from rainfall should be okay, but not when they are a few days old. The exception is desert tanks. These are catchbasins in rocks where water accumulates during rain and remains for as long as months. It is usually quite pure. But watch out for poisoned wells. There are natural pools contaminated with poisons such as arsenic, which look and smell fine, but are deadly. If there are bones lying near a pool, or dead animals or insects in it, do not drink it.

In general, any water you are not completely certain is clean should be filtered or purified. Boiling for ten minutes, or treatment with iodine, will kill any harmful bacteria, but minerals and chemicals can only be removed by distilling or by a purifier. Most campgrounds that have water treat it with chlorine. Some have hand-pump wells or a pipe hammered into a hillside to tap a spring. All campground waters are supposed to be tested at least monthly, so you can be confident they harbor no pathogens; you will not get sick from it. But water from wells and springs is not treated; if you store it for a few days, it is likely to grow algae. It probably won't make you sick, but it becomes off-color and it may taste or smell odd.

Always top off your water when you have a chance, and replace well and spring water at the first opportunity.

Never get contaminated water in your mouth if you can avoid it. You do not have to swallow it to get infected; sometimes just wetting your lips is enough. Water can be contaminated by toxic chemicals or. Bacterial contamination can be handled by boiling or by treatment with iodine or other chemicals, but not chemical contamination. A better handling is a water treatment device. These are often called "purifiers", but most are not. Purifiers remove the toxic chemicals, such as arsenic and salts, and nitrates and nitrites. Water treatments and filters remove only bacteria and some chemicals. You need a real purifier such as micropore carbon. There are many available, such as the Berkey line, ranging from two-gallon drip systems down to little tubes the size of drinking straws. Whatever you get, check the specifications to make sure it is a purifier, not just a filter. Do not depend on what store salesmen say; they often do not know (and won't admit it), and many of them will say anything just to make a sale.

Camping

Where to go

Wherever you want. The options are almost unlimited. My favorites are public lands: National Forests, Monuments and Parks and Bureau of Land Management (BLM) lands, and New Mexico State Parks. Most State Parks and commercial campgrounds such as KOA are too expensive and too developed, intended for people who want to "go camping" and still have all of their comforts and luxuries. It is like the difference between fresh carrots and canned carrots.

There are over 150 National Forests in the US, comprising some 190 million acres. That is bigger than Texas. There are thousands of campgrounds, mostly charging reasonable fees, mostly providing water, trash disposal and toilets of some sort. Usually there is firewood available (for sale and free to gather yourself) and fire rings for your campfires. That is all you really need. You can also camp pretty much anywhere else (dispersed camping) for free in most forests. Some have restrictions on where you can camp, and on how long you can stay at one spot, or how long you can stay in that forest. Some allow two weeks in one campground, then you must move, but it may be to another campground in the same forest. Some allow two weeks in any 45-day period, or in any 90-day period, meaning you can stay in their campgrounds for two weeks, but then must leave the forest for 31 or 76 days. One forest I know of allows only 30 days camping in any calendar year. You can find details for any forest on the internet; just search on National Forest. Excellent maps are available at ranger stations and online, usually ten dollars apiece. They show where the campgrounds and ranger stations are, and what facilities are available. Stop at ranger stations when you can to get the latest updates and to find what areas are open for dispersed camping.

The BLM manages some 245 million acres of public land, mostly in the West, including some National Monuments. Most of it is open for dispersed camping, and there are also campgrounds with facilities. Most of it has a two-week limit on stays, whether dispersed or in campgrounds. Many maps are available online. There is also an excellent book, "Adventures on Public Lands", which details many fine spots and the regulations applying to them.

National Monuments are anything a President decides to label as such, and may be managed by any of several government agencies. For our purposes, they are the same as National Forests. For example, the San Gabriel Mountains National Monument north of Los Angeles used to be most of the Angeles National Forest. It was renamed, but of course it is still the same land and the same campgrounds. Just under new management.

National Parks are essentially that: Parks. Most have campgrounds, and no dispersed camping is allowed. I usually steer clear of them. I may pass through, or camp outside and take a day trip to see the sights (which are well worth seeing!), but their campgrounds are generally crowded and expensive. These are where city people go.

State Parks are usually a lot like National Parks; crowded and expensive. I try to avoid them, but they can be convenient overnight stops, such as when going from Wisconsin to the Rockies. The exception is New Mexico. They cost ten dollars a night, or you can get an annual pass for $225. I detail them in the section on Winter Camping.

You can camp on private land if you first get permission from the owner. I have never needed to do so. Mostly, I stay in National Forests, New Mexico State Parks, and BLM land.

The Campsite

Never arrive at a campground on Friday or Saturday, nor on the day before a holiday, because they often are full. Also never count on a National Park campground, as they are often full all week long. If you really want to stay in a National Park, make a reservation. Most campers are up for the weekend, and arrive Friday afternoon or evening. Clever ones send one person ahead to arrive on Friday morning or even Thursday evening. They tend to leave fairly early (checkout time is usually 2:00 PM), so arriving Sunday afternoon is usually safe. Tuesday and Wednesday arrivals are best; you will almost never find a campground full on those days, and usually there are many sites open, so you can pick a good one. If you plan to stay over the weekend, you may find all of the sites available now, but reserved for the weekend. If you arrive on Tuesday, you can stay overnight, then go find another campground the next day.

Arrive early so you have enough time to set up camp well before dark. If you plan to have a fire, allow enough time to find and gather the wood.

Pick your site with care. You need a good flat spot large enough for your tent, and far enough from the fire that flying sparks are unlikely to reach it. In bear country, if there are not bear-proof food lockers, you want a site on the downwind edge of the campground, where you can easily get to a tree suitable for hanging your food. From an edge site you will also have closer access to the forests for hikes and for gathering firewood. The farther you are from other campsites, the quieter it will be, and the more wildlife you will see. This is getting to be more important with all of these rolling apartments around; they often run generators. If there is a "tents only" section, it is usually the quietest area. Avoid being downwind of the toilets. Check out the trees around you and note what the shade will be like during the whole day. If you carry a solar panel and want to charge something, make sure you can get plenty of direct sunlight. The distance to the nearest water source is not too important. It is convenient to have one nearby, but if it is too far to comfortably carry the water on foot, you can always carry it on your bike.

Keep your camp clean and neat. Wash dishes and stow your food before going to bed, otherwise the night critters will get to them, among whom may be bears.

If you plan to leave early, do as much packing and clean-up as you can the day before.

Campfires

Fire Safety

The worst thing you can do in the forest or grasslands is to start a wildfire. Besides the terrible damage done, you also endanger lives. If you start a wildfire, you can be billed for the costs of suppressing it and of damage done. If someone is killed, you can be charged with manslaughter. I know people who have done it, and are now banned from all National Forests, Parks and Monuments. Banned for life.

Never light a fire:
- When fire danger is extreme.
- When there is a strong wind blowing.
- When fire danger is high and there is any wind more than a light breeze blowing.

- When you have little or no water available to drown it when you are through.

Use your camp stove instead.

Always:
- Prepare the ground to prevent accidental spread.
- Have a bucket of water, or pots and jugs, handy.
- Keep a good shovel at hand to smother sparks.

If fire danger is low and there is little or no wind, and none expected, you do not need to drown your fire before going to bed, but in all other conditions, and always when you leave the camp, even for only five minutes, drown the fire. Pour water over it, stir the ashes, and pour on more water, till it is all no more than warm to the touch. Be especially careful of half-burned logs; a spark deep inside can smolder for days, then burst into flame. Drench them well; if possible, submerge them for a minute or more.

Do not build a fire next to a large log, except possibly in a survival situation. The fire will burn into and under the log, and can be almost impossible to extinguish completely. There are cases on record where a hiker tried to put out a cigarette on an old stump, but the ember smoldered and after a few days, started a wildfire.

About Firewood

There is green wood (still growing or recently cut), squaw wood (dead branches still on the trees), and down wood (dead and lying on the ground). The usual rule in camping areas is you can gather "down and dead" wood, meaning no green stuff and no squaw wood. In arid areas, a lot of brush looks dead, but is still alive, just waiting for a bit of rain. Some areas only allow gathering wood from slash piles (piles of branches left by the foresters), requiring that the randomly dropped wood be left as habitat for the forest critters. Some places, such as most National Parks, forbid *any* gathering of wood. Some even forbid possessing local wood, even if you brought it in from elsewhere.

Some wood, such as fir, does burn well when green, but most does not, so leave the green stuff alone. In most National Forests, it is a crime to damage living trees. Besides, doing so ruins the area for other campers. Squaw wood is especially good in wet weather because it is usually dry, or at least drier than any wood on the ground. But it is also a food source for the birds because insects thrive in it. Only use it when in a survival situation. Personally, I would rather break the laws than die.

You can bring wood in with you, but that is rarely practical on a bike. Many people bring lumber scrap, which is excellent for starting fires, and usually easier to split. It is not as esthetic as logs are for a fire to sit around at night, but it is fine for most cooking and for just keeping warm. Many people leave excess firewood when they go, so check nearby campsites, especially on Sunday afternoons. There are often half-burned logs in the fire pits. At tended campgrounds, the camp hosts usually clean out the firepits, so get the wood as soon as the prior folks leave.

Pine needles are about the best thing for starting fires; leaves and pine cones are also pretty good. But do not gather any pine needles or leaves that are part of the duff. Duff is the stuff on the forest floor that is rotting into soil. When rain falls on bare ground, the impact compresses the dust and sand grains together. Very little water gets absorbed; most just runs off. When rain strikes duff, it spatters, then soaks into the ground below. More water is available for the plants, and less erosion occurs. Pine needles on gravel or in the roads is fair game; it will not do any good where it is, and when you gather it, you are actually doing the campground hosts a favor, because they would have to rake it up anyway. Often they will lend you a rake to clean it up. Many will even bring you the stuff they rake up from other campsites. It always pays to get on good terms with the hosts.

Pine cones make good firewood. They burn quickly and hot, so they are great for boiling water or building a quick bed of coals, and for reviving a dying fire. But they burn out very quickly, so they are not much good for an evening fire. Cones that are still closed should be left, because they contain seeds which the wildlife eats; but the cones that are open rarely contain a seed, and also burn much better.

Do not bring any wood, except lumber scraps, from outside the area, from more than about ten miles away. Dead wood often contains insects and bacteria; importing it can spread tree diseases. This applies to store-bought firewood, too, since it is mostly locally gathered. If you buy firewood, buy it in a town near your campsite, or from a campground host.

Gathering Firewood

Always wear heavy leather gloves when cutting wood. They protect you from scratches and stabs, and provide some protection from a strike when your cutter bounces off the wood. It certainly does no harm to wear them.

Most campgrounds are pretty well picked clean of firewood, but if you just ride a mile or two down the road, you can almost always find ample wood. Branches just lying beside the road are best, because taking them saves work for the road crews. Slash piles are the next best source, because that wood is usually fairly recent, and again, if you do not take it, some work crew will eventually have to haul it away. Make sure it is not *too* recent; if it is still green, it will not burn well. If fallen trees can be seen from the road, just find a good place to pull over, and go get it.

The Lonesome Hillbilly

This is a good place to point out a danger of the forests, especially when gathering firewood: Venomous snakes, scorpions, and cornered animals. Slash piles are likely places to find all of them, because small animals will hide in them, and snakes will hunt the animals. When you are gathering firewood, especially in slash piles, wear heavy leather gloves, and look carefully for critters. They will all (except rabid animals) avoid you if given any chance, but if surprised or cornered, will attack.

Avoid rotten wood, and gray pine needles and leaves; it does not burn well. Rotting is a sort of slow burning; the more the wood rots, the more stored energy it loses. The more solid the wood is, the better fire it will make. Branches still attached to fallen trunks are best, because they are not lying on the ground, so they rot more slowly. Cut branches off and lay them aside. Do not cut it up or trim it more than you must till you get it back to camp. When you have as much as you can comfortably carry, lift it to your shoulder and lug it to your bike. Remember that work is harder at high altitude; you can easily become short of breath if you try to carry a load that would be no problem at sea level. If you are hauling it very far, tying it into a bundle will make it a lot easier to carry. Do not drag it, because that tears up the ground and can cause erosion and other damage, such as killing saplings and other small plants. Do not trim it before carrying it. When you have gathered enough for a full load on the bike, *then* you trim it, but just enough to load it. Cut off the branches and twigs, but do not trim more than you must. The idea is to have a compact mass without a lot of air space, so you can carry more wood. Cut everything to five or six foot lengths. Load any logs on the bike first, laying them across the passenger seat in front of the sissy bar. Leave the saddlebags in place, as they effectively make the seat wider, and make the load ride more stably. Tie the larger branches into bundles, then lay them on the bike. If you are alone, you may want to load the branches and then tie them together. Then make bundles of the smaller branches and load them, and last do the twigs. Strap the whole mass together and to the bike (the loading straps for your gear are perfect for this). Make sure the load is stable and secure, and nothing sticks out too far, then ride carefully back to camp. Done skillfully, you can carry a week's supply of wood in one trip. But take it easy the first few loads; it is an acquired skill.

Gather lots of wood. It is no fun to run out, and anything left over can be used by the next folks.

Back in camp, do the real trimming. First select two branches that will make good strong pokers for tending the fire. Stick them in your fire bucket to soak the ends so they do not catch fire in the coals. Select the largest log to use as a chopping block. When chopping wood, you must never let the cutting edge of your axe or machete strike the ground, because that quickly dulls the edge. Place the stick to be cut at a spot where you will want to cut through the log later. Each time the axe cuts through the stick and strikes the chopping block, it cuts the block, and each cut means one stroke saved when you eventually cut up the big log. Then cut the twigs and smaller branches into lengths a foot or so long, and the other branches into about two-foot lengths. Logs can sometimes be left long. Lay a long log across the fire, and when it burns in half, shove the two halves into the fire. Or just put one end in the fire and keep pushing it in as it burns down. If the flames start to spread beyond your fire ring, splash a bit of water on the wood to control it.

Most campgrounds require that wood must be small enough to fit into the fire rings. In those places, or if it fits your preference, chop or saw the logs to convenient length. Everyone who has cut firewood with a hatchet knows that the first chop or two cut deeper than the following chops. I cut as the beaver does, a couple of chops, turn the wood, a couple more, working all of the way around. Sometimes the log cracks about that time. If not, I pick it up and slam it against the ground or over a rock, and it breaks. Either way, I do the job with a third of the effort in a third of the time it would take to just chop, chop, chop till the log is chopped through.

After you have cut all of the wood, gather the chips and pieces of bark, scraps and bits of twigs together; they make excellent fine stuff the lay over your starter material. That is why you do not trim till you have the wood in camp.

When you go hiking, carry your hatchet or machete and gloves, and keep an eye out for wood, and pick up a load on the way back, just before you get to camp. An armload of wood is not heavy, just awkward, and thus very tiring. A couple of large branches are easy to carry on your shoulder, but the same wood, cut up, will make four or five armloads. You can easily carry a dead twelve or fifteen foot spruce on your shoulder, and make three or four fires from it.

Preparing the Ground

If previous campers left a ring, it's good to use it, if it is sited well. The ideal site would be sheltered from wind, and not under nearby branches, as they can dry out and catch fire. Clear away any flammables within at least ten feet of the fire, so sparks and embers that pop out of the fire will not spread. Lay a ring of large rocks to mark the limits of the fire. Do not use rounded river rocks, or any rock that is wet or taken from the water. If they have absorbed water, they may explode and injure or kill you. In a pristine area, dig a shallow pit for the fire, so you can bury the site when you depart and leave no visible trace of your presence. In grass, cut a large sod which you can lay back and cover the site. Do not build a fire under snow-laden branches; the snow will loosen and fall on you and your fire.

The best place for a fire to keep you warm is at the entrance of a shallow cave (NOT inside the cave). You are protected from wind and rain, and the heat will reflect back from behind you. You can reproduce elements of this when you don't have a cave. If you have a cliff or a large boulder or even a snow bank, build a fire so you can sit between the fire and the cliff; reflected heat will warm your back. A tarp or stand of trees upwind will keep the wind off you. A tarp overhead will keep off rain, but don't build a fire directly under the tarp. You can build a fire next to a large rock to reflect heat, or use a large log or a wall of smaller logs. However, if you do build a fire next to a large log, be very careful to dig out and extinguish all coals before you leave. Coals in a log can smolder for days, then break out and cause a wildfire. A fire on loam or duff can spread underneath, smolder for days, then break out. This is why you must clear the ground down the rock or bare dirt before building a fire.

Laying out the Fire

Lay out the fire so the point where you light it is on the upwind side. Lay the igniter loosely; use dry grass, leaves or pine needles, paper or shredded bark. Lay fine twigs on top, then a frame or tepee of larger twigs, 1/8 to 1/4", but not where they will compress the igniter, then larger branches above that. Have ready branches and logs to feed the fire. Light the fire and when it has caught well, lay on the larger wood. If the fuel is damp, you may have to blow on the fire or fan it to get it well started, but once it is going well, you only have to feed it properly to keep it going. Two logs lying together will not burn well; you have to leave a gap between them to allow air flow. A log set directly on the coals will burn slowly; another log laid above it, with air space between it and the coals will burn faster and hotter. If logs are too far apart, they won't heat each other, and will not burn well. If you keep this in mind, you will soon learn from experience how far apart to place them.

The Lonesome Hillbilly

Lighting the Fire

Lighting a fire under good conditions is very easy. You need a very dry igniter (paper, grass, leaves, pine needles, very fine twigs) placed with lots of air space under a pile of sticks that get progressively larger. One touch of flame and it's off. When everything is damp, it gets harder. Then you need a sustained flame that will last till the wood has caught well. A propane torch or a highway flare will almost always get a fire going. A quarter cup of gasoline or kerosene works well, if placed *under* the wood, not poured atop it. (Never pour gasoline or lighter fluid on a burning fire, even just coals.) Two feet of duck tape loosely wadded lights easily even when wet, and burns long and hot. (NOTE: Gorilla Tape does not hold a flame, nor does the brand Duck Tape. The brands that use rubber cement usually burn well.) A small candle, such as a tea candle, placed under wet twigs will dry then light them. (Not a birthday candle; use a 1/2" stick or a tea candle.)

Some people scoff at using "artificial" fire starters, even paper and butane lighters. Ignore them. It is fun to start a fire with flint and steel or a bow drill; it is a useful skill, and one to be proud of. But if half your gear is made of synthetic fiber and you carry plastic sunglasses, a GPS and a cell phone, it is foolish to scorn lighting a fire with a piece of paper.

Always watch out for wind. Even on a calm day, their may be sudden gusts which can carry embers as much as twenty feet or more. If an ember goes flying, watch it and make sure it does not fall in a dangerous place. If it falls in flammable stuff, go put it out at once with water. It can not only start a wildfire, it can ruin your tent or your bike.

Fire for Cooking

For frying or boiling, you want flames. For all other cooking, you need coals.

Some Chinese peasants use dried grass for all cooking. Twisted into a tight "rope", it can burn for quite a while. Similarly, you can use pine needles, leaves and pinecones, chunks of pine or fir bark, or even sheets of newspaper to keep a hot fire going. Sure, you have to keep feeding it, but if you are frying or cooking something like pancakes, you have to sit there and tend the cooking anyway. For boiling, it is more convenient to use a fuel that will flame longer.

For other cooking, such as baking and roasting, start the fire with a good starter such as pine needles and a lot of small branches or pine cones. It will flare up and in a few minutes leave a bed of coals. Feed that with larger branches while it is still flaring, so the branches are burning well when the original stuff gets down to just coals. When the larger branches are mostly coals, you can start cooking. Such a fire is best laid between two large logs, not split. They will keep the coals in the cooking area, and reflect heat inwards, and also act as andirons; fresh branches laid across them, well above the coals, will burn quickly and replenish the bed of coals. Dried dung from cows, horses and bison makes a good long-burning fuel for baking. It does tend to flavor roasted meats. It is not bad for you, but you may not care for the taste.

Pay attention to the size of the fire. Once a pot is boiling, it takes little fire to keep it at a boil. Likewise with frying. Notice how long it takes a new stick to catch fire. Then you can avoid adding wood too soon (fire gets too hot) or too late (fire gets too small). With just a little practice, you can keep a fire always at the same size, which makes cooking easier. If the fire is too large, water will boil away faster, baked and fried foods will burn, roasted food will be done on the outside and still raw in the center, or done in the center and burned on the outside. If the fire is too small, food will take longer to cook, fried foods will absorb more grease, and roasted food will dry out. A large fire will also use up more wood; then you have to work to gather more.

Fire for Warmth

As mentioned in Preparing the Ground, a reflector behind the fire or behind you, or both, will conserve fuel. Gather plenty of wood and then only use what you need so you do not run out. Too big a fire not only wastes wood, it can more easily get away from you. On the other hand, do not use too little. Forget the Hollywood lore that Indians build small fires and sit over them. Small fires are hard to keep burning, and tend to smoke a lot. The fire should be small enough that you can sit close enough to add fuel without getting up, but large enough to keep you comfortably warm. For a large group of people, build two or three fires; they can be as close as about five feet apart, so the groups are close enough for conversation.

Winter Camping

Camping in winter is very different from the other seasons. Weather is harsher. Many areas get snow, some pretty heavy. You do *not* want to do motorcycle camping in snow. Bikes are *way* too fond of snow; they love to lie down and roll in it. You can get tire chains for the bike, and should carry them, because snow can hit the higher elevations at any time, but if you want to camp in snowy areas, you are on your own. I have done it when caught in a late blizzard (*Very* late. In July.) The only advice I can give you is : If you really want to camp in snow, get a trike.

But there are areas that get little or no snow in winter, such as Southwest Arizona and Texas. If you are motorcycle camping in winter, the best place is Southern New Mexico. I camp year-round. I have a storage shed where I keep some non-camping stuff, and spare gear. I visit it in April and September, and swap out summer and winter gear. The winter gear includes electric stuff. You see, New Mexico has more than thirty State Parks, and they are the best state parks in the country. Camping is ten dollars per night for a site with water, a fire ring, and usually a ramada or similar roof shelter over a picnic table. Nearby is a building with flush toilets and, usually, hot showers. Free hot showers. This is *very* attractive for long-term campers. Most sites also have electric outlets, for an extra four dollars per night. Some also have sewer hookups (which you won't need) for another four dollars. If you have to take a full-hookup site, there being no others unoccupied, you pay the full eighteen dollars, even though you won't use the hook-ups. However, you can buy an annual permit for $225. This covers the ten dollar camping fee. If you pick an electric site, you only pay the four dollar part of the fee. If you stay in New Mexico for the full mountain snow season, about November to April, you can do 180 days worth $2,520 ($1,800 camping fee, $720 electricity fee) for $945, or $5.25 per day. You get a campsite, water, toilets, showers, and electricity. Some of the parks also have free WiFi.

So, what is different about winter camping? The weather is colder, often sub-freezing, and the wind is generally stronger. Plastic dome tents are difficult or impossible to heat, and tend to flatten out in winds over 35 MPH. A good canvas tent can be heated, and should stand up to any normal wind; mine has weathered 60 MPH gusts with no problems. You can rig such a tent with a hole for a small chimney, and heat it with a gas or wood stove, or use an electric heater when you have electricity. You are not going to heat it to a toasty 72 degrees, but you can get it to a comfortable level, at least with a sweater and/or jacket.

Snow can accumulate on the tent. A plastic tent is likely to collapse; a canvas tent is more likely to hold up till morning, when you can clean the snow off.

Rain is more common, and much colder than in other seasons. You should have very good and comfortable rain gear, and waterproof boots. You will need heavy riding gear: Waterproof insulated gloves and pants, waterproof boots or boot covers, and a riding jacket with a quilted liner. You can also get electrically heated gloves and suit. The waterproof aspect is mostly for windproofing.

You will need more firewood, and you must have a cover for it to keep it dry.

When camping in New Mexico in winter, where electricity is available, I carry some extra gear:

- Slow Cooker
- Hot plate
- Electric heater
- 100 foot extension cord

A 100' cord is not heavy or too bulky, and allows you a much greater selection of tent sites. This can be very important. The campsites are laid out for RVs, which usually have their electric hook-up on the left side, and the door on the right. This means electric outlets at campsites are rarely located in a good position for tent camping.

A slow cooker is excellent for camp cooking. For one thing, you can load it in the evening with a breakfast, such as black-eye peas and bacon, and let it cook all night inside the tent. It keeps the tent a bit warmer, and you wake up to a hot meal all ready to eat.

A hot plate is suitable for pancakes or eggs or whatever, and can be used inside the tent, out of the wind. Of course, you lose the chance to sit by the fire, but only for that meal. You can still have a campfire whenever you want.

Camping Tips and Tricks

Ticks
These can be very dangerous, especially in the Rocky Mountains, where they carry diseases. Check for ticks at least daily during spring, summer and fall. You will usually find them among hair and around your waist, but they may bite anywhere. Do not pull them off, for you may pull off the head, which will infect the wound. The best way to remove a tick is with a lighted cigarette or a glowing coal on the end of a twig, which makes them let go. You can also touch them with a drop of alcohol, lighter fluid, gasoline or kerosene. They will usually let go, but if they do not, it kills them and they relax their grip so you can pull them off with less chance of leaving the head behind.

Insect Repellent
If you travel in mosquito country, you need an insect repellent. There are many commercial ones available, and some of them work, more or less. I do not buy them. Nessmuk, a woodsman of the late 19th century, made a very effective repellent, which I have used, and have never found a better one. He described it in his book "Woodcraft", and I reproduce it here, verbatim:

"It was published in Forest and Stream in the summer of 1880 and again in '83. It has been pretty widely quoted and adopted and I have never known it to fail: Three ounces pine tar, two ounces castor oil, one ounce pennyroyal oil. Simmer all together over a slow fire and bottle for use. You will hardly need more than a two-ounce vial full in a season. One ounce has lasted me

The Lonesome Hillbilly

six weeks in the woods. Rub it in thoroughly and liberally at first, and after you have established a good glaze, a little replenishing from day to day will be sufficient. And don't fool with soap and towels where insects are plenty. A good safe coat of this varnish grows better the longer it is kept on--and it is cleanly and wholesome. If you get your face and hands crocky or smutty about the campfire, wet the corner of your handkerchief and rub it off, not forgetting to apply the varnish at once, wherever you have cleaned it off. Last summer I carried a cake of soap and a towel in my knapsack through the North Woods for a seven weeks' tour and never used either a single time. When I had established a good glaze on the skin, it was too valuable to be sacrificed for any weak whim connected with soap and water. When I struck a woodland hotel, I found soap and towels plenty enough. I found the mixture gave one's face the ruddy tanned look supposed to be indicative of health and hard muscle. A thorough ablution in the public wash basin reduced the color, but left the skin very soft and smooth; in fact, as a lotion for the skin it is excellent. It is a soothing and healing application for poisonous bites already received."

It is all true. It is the most effective insect repellent I know of, and it is good for the skin. It does not stink like commercial products. You can buy the ingredients at Amazon. $50 buys enough pine tar for eleven batches, castor oil for eight and pennyroyal oil for two. It works out to $1.42 per ounce, and one six-ounce batch is $8.52. I wash a bit more often than Nessmuk did, but I am not often in mosquito country. Six ounces lasts me about a year. I carry it in a stainless steel hip liquor flask.

Mosquito Bites
If a mosquito does get through your defenses and bite you, it can itch for days. Or you can clean it by squeezing out the poison. First you pinch the bite, hard, to squeeze the sides together and open the entry hole in the center. Then you use the edge of a

fingernail or a spoon or something similar to push the toxins toward the hole and out. Starting no more than ½ inch from the hole, press the skin and slide toward the hole Work around in a circle several times. You will usually see a sort of oily wetness forming at the hole. The treated bite will be sore for a minute or so, but that will be the end of it; no more itching.

Scorpions
These are common in the American deserts, and in some other areas as well. The large ones, two inches and more, can give you a very nasty and painful sting, but are rarely deadly to a healthy adult. Pets, small children and people with heart conditions are much more at risk. The little ones, just an inch or so long, are truly deadly.

When camping in scorpion country, always keep the lower half of your tent door zipped up, so scorpions cannot crawl in and into, say, your bedding. As far as is feasible, keep all of your gear inside the tent. If you pick up a tarp or bag that has been lying on the ground, check it for scorpions, and shake it out to make sure there are none. Before putting on shoes or boots, turn them upside down and shake them, and knock the soles hard to shake loose any bugs inside. Look inside as far as you can.

Rattlesnakes
Bites from most snakes, including rattlesnakes, are much like stings from large scorpions, painful and debilitating, but generally not fatal. Water moccasins and coral snakes are a couple of exceptions, but I am really only familiar with Western snakes. But even non-fatal bite should be strongly avoided. That is pretty easy. Watch the ground where you are going, check for snakes before reaching into a bush or picking up firewood, do not step over a log or large rock without looking first. (The Boy Scout Handbook says to step *on* logs and rocks, not over them, to avoid snakebite. It used to say step *over* them because they might

roll or break under your foot.) Walk noisily. Don't exactly stomp your feet, but do make noise, snap twigs and kick small rocks. The snakes hear vibrations through their bellies, and if given a chance, will get out of your way. They do not want to bite you; you are too big to eat.

Take the same tent precautions as you would for scorpions. Snakes are known to crawl into a warm sleeping bag with the camper.

Other Venomous Critters
There are also gila monsters and black widow spiders and brown spiders and other nasties. The same precautions that you take for scorpions and rattlesnakes will do for the rest. For example, I always clear out my shoes, even if I am not in scorpion country.

Passes
National Parks and Forests have Interagency Passes, most of them good for a year, and provide several discounts. It is government stuff, so what they cover may change at any time. Check them out and get the best one you qualify for. If you are 62 or older, get the Golden Age pass. At this time it costs ten dollars and never expires, covers all National Park entry fees, and usually is good for a 50% discount on campground fees. While most National Parks are no longer good places to camp (way too crowded), often your best route leads through a park. Without the pass, you may pay twenty or thirty dollars just to pass through. Have the pass and your ID ready before you approach the gate.

Hygiene
Change socks and underwear daily; you can wash them by hand now and then, so you do not have to carry fifteen pair of each. Wash your feet and groin daily, and armpits if you get sweaty. If you are hiking, use foot powder; it is not important if you are staying around the camp or riding. Pants and shirts you can

usually wear for a week or more, if you do not sweat too much. A full shower every week or so is usually sufficient. Get a solar shower bag. The least expensive I have found is Ozark Trails, about nine dollars at Wal-Mart. It is just as effective as the expensive ones, and should last at least through a long trip if not handled roughly. To use it, you fill it with water and lay it in direct sunlight for a few hours; I lay it out first thing in the morning for an afternoon shower. Toss a rope over a branch at least ten feet high. Clip a small pulley to the end of the rope and pass a 1/4 inch line through it. Raise the pulley to the branch. When you are ready for the shower, test the water to make sure it is not too hot, and add a bit of cold if necessary. Attach the bag to the line and haul it up to where you can just reach the valve on the bag. Use just enough water to get yourself wet, then scrub down. You do not always need soap, but when you do use it, get a bio-friendly type. Castile soap or coal tar soap or Ivory Soap is good. You can buy (expensive) camp soaps at sporting goods stores. You can also use wood ashes, or make soap from ashes and fat such as lard or olive oil. After you scrub, rinse off with the rest of the water. Drain the bag completely and take it down; if you leave it hanging with water in it, you will wear it out sooner.

Cat-holes and Slit Trenches
When doing dispersed camping, there is usually no toilet available. What do you do? Dig a hole about a foot deep. Use it. Throw in a couple of handfuls of dirt, then use a short stick to mix the dirt and excrement well, so they will decompose faster. Leave the stick in the hole and fill it in. Tamp it down well. If you are going to camp there for more than a day, dig a slit trench. It is about six to eight inches wide, at least a foot deep, and a couple of feet long; the longer you stay, the longer the trench needs to be. Leave the shovel by the trench. Squat at one end to use it, and when you are done, toss in some dirt and stir it with a short stick, drop the stick on top, and bury it enough to hold in the

smells. Move a few inches farther on each time you use it. When you leave, fill it in and tamp it down well.

There is a lot of talk about packing out used toilet paper. The argument is that it takes a long time to decompose. Right. It takes longer for down wood to decompose. As long as it is stirred and well buried, I see no problem.

If you cannot bury it, like in winter when the ground is frozen solid, sure, pack it out. If you disagree with me and want to pack it out all of the time, go ahead. Get two sealable plastic bags such as zip-locks. Put one inside the other and add a teaspoon or so of dry bleach or borax powder or a tablespoon of baking soda (or three of baking powder) for a deodorant. Stuff the paper in the inner bag and seal both, squeezing out most of the air.

Keeping Cool
If it is hot and dry and you have plenty of water available, a wet t-shirt and head rag will keep you comfortable even if there is no breeze. If it is humid this does not work as well, but pouring cool water over yourself will help a lot. Go swimming. Lie down in a stream. Keep a wet cloth on the back of your neck. Wear a wide-brim hat, with a ventilated crown. Seek shade and drink lots of water or fruit juice. Gator-Ade is easily the best sports drink, because it was designed solely to handle dehydration. All of the others were designed to cash in on the Gator-Ade market. Sodas and beer are not good for preventing dehydration. Make sure you eat enough salt. There is a big superstition these days about salt and how bad it is for you. Like everything else, too much is bad, but not enough is worse. If a potato chip or something else salty tastes especially good, you need salt. You can buy (expensive) salt tablets, or you can dissolve a teaspoon of salt in a cup of water and chug it. If you are feeling dizzy or faint on a hot day or when you have been sweating a lot, you probably need salt. In hot weather, it is a good idea to carry cell salts.

Keeping Warm

First rule: Keep everything dry; dampness makes cold feel much worse, and cold when you are wet can kill you. Several thin layers of clothing are better than one thick one. Wool will still keep you warm when it is wet, where cotton and synthetics will not. Woolen long underwear is the best first layer. Silk is the best inner layer when you will be sweating in the cold, because it wicks sweat away. In freezing temperatures, *avoid sweating!* When you stop moving and cool off, the sweat can freeze next to your skin. It is *very* dangerous. Over your wool underwear, wear a couple of t-shirts, then thicker shirts such as denim or felt. Wool felt shirts are best. Thermal long underwear is very good, as long as it is not wet, or you are wearing an inner layer of wool. Denim or canvas long pants are best for the outer layer. Over that you can wear a coat or a parka. Of course, in rain or snow, a waterproof outer layer is needed. You may have noticed that woodsmen usually wear baggy clothes. Your shirt and pants need to be a couple of sizes large so they will fit over the inner layers.

Keep your head covered. A balaclava or ski mask is perfect for wear when sleeping. For your feet, wear silk socks then a pair or two of thick woolen socks and a waterproof boot. On your hands, silk gloves, wool gloves, and waterproof gloves. A sleeping bag must be insulated from the ground, because the ground is cold and will suck the heat right through your bag. An air mattress is good, a tough plastic foam pad is better. A layer of leaves or pine needles is effective, and even a blanket will help. A blanket over your sleeping bag will also make a noticeable difference.

Of course, both Keeping Cool and Keeping Warm are written about extremes. For in-between temperatures, the same principles apply, just not as much.

The Lonesome Hillbilly

Keeping Things Cool

First, keep stuff out of direct sunlight, of course. This includes your ice chest or cooler, if you carry one. Coolers do not keep heat out, they only slow it down, so keep the cooler in the coolest place available. If there is plenty of water available, wrap bottles in absorbent cloth such as a T-shirt or towel soaked in water. Keep it wet, and the evaporation will cool the stuff down in about half an hour, and keep it cool. Wrapping your sleeping bag around cold stuff first thing in the morning will keep it cool for most of the day. Waterproof containers sitting in a stream will cool quickly.

Multi-Use Gear

You need to keep weight and bulk down; when one thing does two or three jobs, you have less to carry. For example, a hatchet will serve as a hammer. A balaclava will serve as a helmet liner, and also as a nightcap. A solar shower can be used to haul drinking water, as a kitchen sink faucet, and a sprinkler for dousing the campfire. A multi-tool pocket knife with can opener and corkscrew blades means you don't need to carry a separate can opener and corkscrew, and will also serve as an eating knife. In fact, it replaces half a toolbox full of other tools. Your sheath knife will do fine as a carving knife. Always keep multi-use in mind when selecting gear.

Things You Need to Know
- Knots: Know how to tie a bowline, square knot, and clove hitch. It is also good to know the figure-eight knot, trucker's hitch, hunter's bend, and whipping and splicing.
- Sewing: You do not have to be good at it, just enough to be able to stick things together. Of course, the better you can sew, the more use it will be.
- First Aid: Take a basic Red Cross course, or study a good reference book.

- Cooking: The better you can cook, the more you will enjoy the trip.
- Mileage: Know how far you can go before you have to switch to Reserve, and how far you can go before the tank runs dry. Know you mileage on mountain roads, on city streets, and on highways at 50, 60, 70 MPH.
- Finding direction: How to locate north. At night, there are several star configurations that point north. In the day, mark a shadow on the ground and wait fifteen minutes, then mark it again; a line connecting the two marks will point east and west. Moss is not reliable. It does grow on the north side of trees (and highway workers), but is usually grows on other sides as well.
- Basic bike repairs: Even if you have roadside assistance such as AAA, you will often be in areas where there is no cell phone reception. Then you have to do it yourself, or trust to luck that someone will come along to help or to relay a message for you.

Campfire Cooking

Have you ever read a book about campfire cooking? They are mostly regular kitchen recipes, with a lot of forest history and anecdotes to pad them out. This is because there is not much to say about the subject, and few recipes that are actually designed for camping. I will tell you the basics of fires and food, of pots and pans, so you can avoid burning your meals and yourself. Then you can easily adapt most recipes to the campfire. I will also add a few recipes and ideas that only apply to campfires.

Camp Stove vs. Camp Fire
Sometimes you cannot have a campfire. Then you have to use a camp stove, or else not cook. If you are just out for a weekend or a week, you may not want to bother with cooking at all. But if you are a coffee drinker, you should have a stove of some type. Propane or butane stoves are common. You can get small single-burners that screw on to a gas cylinder, and are very cheap. You can get a two- or three- burner stove, but now we are getting into cost and weight. It would be a good idea if you are in a group, say four or more, so one person carries the stove and the others share out other gear. You can also get a liquid-fuel stove. The stove cost is about the same, and the white gas they burn costs about the same per hour of cooking as gas cylinders. But gas cylinders are somewhat more common in stores. I use a dual-fuel stove that burns unleaded gas, so I can use my spare gas can to fill it. The gas is a lot cheaper, and available everywhere.

Whichever stove you choose, it must be used in a well-ventilated area. A plastic dome tent is usually half mosquito netting, so the ventilation is good, but they are flammable, and melt very easily. I do *not* recommend using any stove inside one. A canvas tent would be okay, *if* it is well ventilated. In fact, the only real advantage to using the stove in a tent is to keep it out of wind and rain. A fair wind, say 20 MPH or more, slows down cooking to a very large extent. If the wind is blowing, put up some kind of wind barrier. Cook on the downwind side of your tent, or make a wall of cardboard or boxes or duffel bags, anything to shelter the stove. Other than that, there is not much to say about camp stoves.

Campfires are more complex, more work, and a lot more fun. One of the greatest pleasures of camping is the hot fire on a cold morning! They also have the advantage of allowing more ways to cook. It is hard to bake, and almost impossible to roast or barbecue on a camp stove, and as for toasting marshmallows...

How to build a fire for cooking is explained in the Campfires section. The most important point to remember is that campfires are hotter than you think they are; burned food is the most common outdoor mistake. You can get a good-enough measure of the temperature by holding your hand about five inches above where the pan will be, and counting seconds till you have to pull your hand away before it hurts.

8-10 seconds means low heat, 250-350 degrees F
5-7 seconds means medium heat, 350-450 degrees F
2 to 4 seconds means high heat, 450-550 degrees F

Once you have built the base fire and have a good bed of coals, you need to modify the fire for the type of cooking you will do. The heat rises straight up in calm air, but any wind will waft the heat downwind, and you want to position the pan where the heat is; the stronger the wind, the farther downwind you should shift the pan. When tending the pans, stay upwind of the fire to keep cooler and out of the smoke. I know, it seems an obvious thing, but I see many people doing it wrongly.

The Lonesome Hillbilly

Boiling and Simmering
For boiling and long simmering, put your grill in place as soon as the fuel has burned down far enough to let it fit. Set the pot of water on it to take advantage of the remaining flare. Feed the fire to keep the flames licking at the bottom of the pot; always have a couple of two or three inch sticks burning, and use smaller ones to keep the flames up. Once the water is boiling, let the flames die down. Only add enough wood to keep the water boiling; it does not take much heat. For a long slow simmer, such as cooking chile or beans, you only need to see two or three bubbles per second. A covered pot requires less heat to stay up to temperature. You cannot see the bubbles, but there will be a small wisp of steam escaping. If you have not built a smoky fire, you can see the steam. If the lid is wobbling, the fire is too hot. If a *cast iron* lid is wobbling, the fire is *way* too hot!

The boiling point of water decreases with altitude, about two degree Fahrenheit, or 1.1 Celsius, for every thousand feet.

Frying and Sauteeing
For frying, you want a bit more heat; keep the flames licking at the pan all of the time. For sauteeing, not so much, about the same as for maintaining a boil. For some things, such as fried eggs or pancakes, you will be sitting at the fire constantly, so try using just pine needles. Often you can get big piles of them (but see the cautions in the Firewood section). A bushel is more than enough for breakfast for two. Start the fire with pine needles and some pinecones or small sticks to build a small bed of coals. Then add a small handful of needles at a time, whenever the flames start to die. (IMPORTANT: I said *start* to die; you need enough flame left to start the new needles burning at once, so you keep a steady heat.) By adding needles about once, maybe twice a minute, the heat will be kept just right for pancakes. You will not be too busy. In fact, I find it a bit boring to pour batter then wait seventy seconds before flipping the pancakes. Tending the

fire passes the time. And by the time you have finished eating, the fire is burned out, nothing left but ashes.

Roasting

For roasting, you need a big bed of coals. You start the fire the same as any other, but if you can, first set up a reflector on the upwind side. A large flat rock set close to vertical is best. Or you can drive two stakes in the ground about thirty degrees off the vertical, leaning away from the fire, then stack green logs (not ash wood or pitch pine or other wood that burns when green), six or eight inch diameter and about four feet long, against the sticks to make a wall two to three feet tall. Build the fire at the base of the reflector, and cook on the downwind side. While the base fire is flaring, add extra large sticks, two to four inch size, so they become coals. Add wood to the upwind side and push the resulting coals to the middle to maintain the heat. Roasting directly over the coals tends to cook the meat too fast and dry it out. Do not place the meat there unless you will be basting often, such as with a barbecue sauce. Set the meat beside the fire. The slower meat roasts, the more tender and juicy it will be. Also, if you roast it too fast, the outside will be burned while the inside is still cold. Turn the meat frequently.

Planking

Planking is a special form of roasting which can only be done on a fire. You pin the meat to a flat piece of wood and face it to the fire. The wood does not have to be smooth, just flat. The texture of a split cedar shingle is perfect. You must use a pleasant tasting wood such as cedar (the best) or apple. Do not use a resinous wood such as pine or fir.

Baking

Baking requires coals, lots of them. It is best done in cast iron, in a dutch oven or a frying pan with a cover. The pan is placed on the coals, with more coals piled on top.

As with anything else, campfire cooking takes practice. After cooking a dozen or so meals, you should get the hang of it. Too much heat cooks too fast and burns you and the food, and makes you rush when tending the pans. Smoke makes you rush, too, when it gets in your eyes and chokes you. Long-handled utensils and long sleeves help a lot. Leather gloves keep your hands from scorching and let you touch and push hot pans, but for picking up a hot pan, you need more insulation; a folded bandanna works well.

High Altitude Cooking

Above 2,500 feet, cooking is a bit different from sea-level cooking. The main reason is the lower atmospheric pressure due to a thinner blanket of air above. The air pressure decreases about a half pound for each 1,000 feet. At sea level air pressure is 14.7 pounds; at 5,000 feet it is 12.3 pounds; at 10,000 feet it is 10.2 pounds. Since the air pressure is lower, the boiling point of water is lower, so cooking takes longer. Since the air is also drier, moisture evaporates more quickly from everything, so food may come out dry. Covering foods during cooking will help retain moisture. Water also evaporates faster at lower temperatures, and this affects *all* food. I have taken fresh bread out of its wrapper and by the time I have finished making a sandwich, the bread was dried out. Any foods that can dry out should be kept covered as much as possible.

For every 500-foot increase in elevation, the boiling temperature of water drops by about 1 degree F. At sea level, water boils at 212 degrees F. At 7,500 feet, water boils at about 198 degrees F. Food being cooked in water or by moist heat doesn't get as hot, so it has to be cooked for a longer time. Thus there is more time for evaporation to occur during cooking, which can cause food to dry out.

At altitudes above 2,500 feet, preparation of food may require changes in time, temperature or recipe. Turning up the heat will not help cook food faster except when using dry heat, such as roasting, broiling and baking. No matter how high the cooking temperature, water cannot exceed its own boiling point. Even a pressure cooker will be cooking at a lower temperature. If the heat is turned up, the water will simply boil away faster and whatever you are cooking will dry out faster. Most sea-level recipes work up to around 2,500 to 3,000 feet. If you go higher, they usually require some adjustment.

To make this less complicated, I will write of adjustments for a 5,000 foot altitude. If you are higher, the adjustments will be greater. If you are lower, the adjustments will be lesser.

Boiling and Simmering
The higher the altitude, the lower the boiling point of water, so the longer it will take to boil and simmer foods. Cook pasta and noodles *al dente*; they will take as much as five minutes longer.

Soups and stews will need more liquid because they are cooking longer, so keep a closer eye on it till you get the feel. You may need as much as 25% more liquid.

When making rice, add 15% to 20% more liquid and cook a few extra minutes. Use my recipe at the end of the book, and you will run no risk of scorching the rice.

Grilling, Roasting and Broiling
Since the lower air pressure means water evaporates faster, when grilling or roasting, you will need to cook longer. You will also need to baste more often, especially the last five or ten minutes. Depending on the density and size of the pieces, meats and poultry cooked by dry or moist heat may take up to one-fourth more cooking time when cooked at 5,000 feet.

If you are cooking in an oven (including a dutch oven), the sea-level temperature guidelines are accurate, because the oven temperatures are not affected by altitude changes. However, the lower boiling point still applies, so it will take longer and you will have to baste more often.

At high altitudes, it is easy to overcook meat and poultry or scorch casseroles. A food thermometer is very useful. They are small and light, and measure the only factor of importance in determining when meat is done. The instant-read type is preferable, especially when cooking thin foods, such as pork chops and hamburgers. Regardless of the air pressure or evaporation rate, when beef reaches 140 degrees F or chicken reaches 165 degrees F, it is as done as it would be at sea level.

When taking the temperature of any meat, or casseroles and other made dishes, the food thermometer should be placed in the thickest part of the meat, avoiding bone and fat. The thermometer should be inserted in the side of the food so that the entire sensing area (usually 2-3 inches) is positioned through the center of the food.

For a whole bird, check the internal temperature in the innermost part of the thigh and at the thickest part of the breast. If you stuff whole poultry, also check the center of the stuffing.

As to what temperature you should cook to, I make no recommendations; the "official" numbers keep changing. Use the same temperatures you use at home.

Eggs take longer to cook at high altitudes, especially poached and hard-cooked eggs because water boils at a lower temperature than it does at sea level. Do not increase the heat, just increase the cooking time. On the other hand, eggs baked in the shell in dry heat take exactly as long as at sea level.

Deep-Fat Frying

Deep-fat frying cooks by boiling the water in foods. You need to lower the temperature of the fat to prevent food from over-cooking on the outside while being under-cooked on the inside. The decrease varies somewhat according to the food being fried, but a rough guide is to lower the frying temperature about 3 degrees F for every increase of 1,000 feet in elevation.

Slow Cooker

At high altitudes, slow cookers simmer at a lower temperature. However, the cooker does not know the altitude, just the temperature, so you need to cook longer, and add extra water. Remember that if you remove the lid from the slow cooker, you add a good 20 minutes or longer to the cooking time; add the extra water at the start.

You can set the slow cooker to high for the first hour to get the food up to temperature faster, then either continue on high or switch to low.

Use a food thermometer to confirm that the food is done.

Pressure Cooker

You might think a pressure cooker would not be affected by the altitude change, but it is. Sure, the internal pressure still reaches 15 pounds, but this is the *difference* between the internal and external temperatures. At sea level, you have 14.7 pounds pressure, so the *actual* pressure inside is 29.7 pounds. At 5000 feet, you are starting with only 12.3 pounds, so the pressure cooker only gets up to 27.3 pounds. The boiling point is higher inside the cooker, but it is still ten degrees lower than it would be at sea level. And thus, you still have to increase the cooking time by about the same percentage as you must for boiling something, such as pasta. Not the same amount of time, or number of minutes; the same *percentage* of time.

Most pressure cookers only have one weighted gauge, so all you can do is increase the cooking time. If your pressure cooker has more than one weight, you can adjust it by using a larger weight. If you can adjust it so the internal pressure is the same as it would be at sea level, then you can use the exact same times for cooking as you would use at sea level. Just be sure you follow the manufacturer's directions.

Until you are familiar with the amount of change needed, use a meat thermometer to make sure the food is done.

Baking
About the only baking I do is bannock, corn bread and potatos, so I am no expert. The following data I have assembled by research on several internet sites, Government, University, and Private.

The main factor affecting baked items is the low pressure, which causes lower boiling point, faster evaporation, and faster rising, and will also dry ingredients, which gives the baked goods a dry and crumbly texture. There are half a dozen adjustments you can make, and they interact with each other, and also work somewhat differently for different recipes. And to make it even worse, there are many microclimates in the mountains, so the adjustment that works for you at one campsite may not work at another one at the same altitude, but only a couple of miles away. I never do any complicated baking while camping, and I do not expect you will, so I will only give a few basics. If you want to learn about high-altitude baking in detail, I suggest you try the Colorado State University Extension Resource Center website. They have a very complete set of publications available.

Baked goods will take longer to cook. Increase either the temperature or the cooking time. Start with one or the other and see how it works.

For baking at elevations up to 5000 ft:
- Increase cooking temperature 15 to 25 degrees F
- Add 2 to 3 tablespoons of water for each cup of liquid (just water, not the liquid itself)
- Decrease sugar by 2 to 3 tablespoons per cup
- Decrease leavening agents by 25%
- Decrease fat by 1 to 2 tablespoons per cup
- Increase flour by 1 to 2 tablespoons per cup

It is recommended you start by trying only one adjustment at a time. Every recipe is different and any or all of these adjustments may be required. If you are above 5000 feet, the adjustments will be greater. Increase them gradually. You will probably use different adjustments for different recipes. Keep notes of how you adjust recipes, along with the altitude.

All-Purpose flour works better than cake flour. Also, flavors in baked goods can become weaker or less pronounced as there is less water to carry them. Adding a bit of extra flavoring will be needed to get the taste you expect.

When a recipe calls for oatmeal, add extra water or use quick oats. Old fashioned oats tend to dry a baked good out faster as they absorb more liquid.

Adding extra egg or use extra large eggs or jumbo eggs.

For any baking that requires folding or whipping, underdo it a little, else it may rise too much and collapse.

Yeast doughs rise quicker at higher altitudes, so punch the dough down an extra time and let it rise again.

Cookware

Pots and Pans
Cast iron is perfect for campfires, because it holds heat and distributes it better than any other material. A thin steel frying pan will always have hot spots, and will burn food in one spot while leaving it raw in another. A couple of stainless steel pots are essential. The big pot is for cooking pasta and soups, especially with acidic ingredients such as tomatos, and for boiling water to disinfect it or for washing up. The smaller pot is for heating up food already cooked, or for rice and corn meal mush, or oatmeal. If you smear a thin layer of dish soap on the outside of the pot before cooking, most soot will not stick to it. I do not do that because the soap itself is messy, and I do not mind having my pots soot-stained. I generally do not scrub off the soot till I am breaking camp and stowing the gear.

For cleaning cookware, a coarse plastic scrubbing pad is very good. Toss in a handful of clean sand and a handful of white wood ash, wet it, and scrub with the pad. The sand scours well, the ashes cut grease. Scrubbing with sand is the best way to clean off soot deposits. Do not use sand or ash on cast iron!

Carry a sack or two for stowing the pots. These sacks should be waterproof, heavy plastic or plasticized canvas. Any grease and soot you do not get off of the pans (and there will be some) can make a mess of your other gear. These sacks will keep the mess enclosed. Most of your cookware, such as dishes and measuring cups and such, will fit inside your pots, and thus take up no space.

Seasoning Cast Iron
Cast iron must be seasoned before use; pre-seasoning is sort of okay for kitchens, but it is *not* seasoning. Scrub your new pan well with hot water and coarse steel wool (and *no soap*) to get off the waxy factory anti-rust coating. Never use soap on cast iron

because the iron will absorb the soap and flavor your food. Never. No soap. Dry the pan thoroughly by heating it. When it cools enough to handle, use a clean cloth to rub in a generous coat of fat. Do not use shortening. Some people say you can get good results with "vegetable" oils, but in my experience, nothing works so well as animal fat. Lard or bacon grease is best, beef and mutton fat also work well. Rub it in generously, inside and out, including the handles and all over the cover. Line the bottom of an oven with aluminum foil to catch drips, then place the pans inside, upside down. This lets excess fat drip out instead of pooling in the bottom. Heat the oven to 350 degrees and leave the pans for five or six hours. It will smoke, so keep the outside doors and windows open. Cool the pots till you can handle them, then rub in lots of fresh fat and bake them again. You can season at a campfire, or in a closed charcoal or gas grill, but an oven is best.

The fat has soaked into the cast iron and burned away leaving a coating of slightly greasy carbon. That is the seasoning. It helps prevent rust, and produces a non-stick surface. The seasoning on the outside, on the bottom, the handle and the cover, is, I suppose, mostly for rust prevention. It is the seasoning on the inside that is important, mainly for the non-stick function. There will often be a little sticking of food, but it usually wipes off easily with a wooden or plastic spatula. Bacon tends to leave the worst deposit, hard to scrape. Anything like that will burn right off. A really dirty pan, such as after cooking bacon, can be left on the fire. Everything in the pan will burn off and can be wiped away. It also continues the seasoning. Or you can add a little water and heat it till it starts to simmer, then wipe the pan clean with a plastic scrubbing pad.

Over time, more bits of food and grease will get into the tiny irregularities of the iron, burn to carbon, and thicken the seasoning. After a couple of years (yes, it takes years), you will have a lining that is as smooth as glass, almost perfectly non-stick, and very easy to cook on. Old-time mountain men treasured that coating, and if some tenderfoot broke that layer with a steel spatula or by washing with soap, the old-timer would break that person's arm. Their campmates would side with the old-timer.

Cleaning and Care of Cast Iron
To clean cast iron safely (safe for the pan as well as for your arm), let it cool a bit, then rinse it with water and wipe it off with a cloth. Paper towels work poorly; they tend to leave tiny bits of paper to flavor your next meal. Never pour water on hot cast iron, as it may warp or crack, and never use steel utensils on it, because they can scratch and ruin the seasoning. Never store them wet, lest they rust, which destroys the seasoning. Damaged seasoning means you have to re-season the pan; there is no repair, you must start fresh. The outside of a frying pan can develop a greasy build-up. That can be scraped off with a metal tool or scoured with coarse steel wool, but not soap. Never soap. After washing, heat up the pan to dry it completely. If you store it for a long time, you are supposed to give it a light coat of oil and leave a dry paper towel inside, if you put the cover on. It sounds right, but I do not know because I have never stored cast-iron; I use it too often. If you carry anything hard inside a cast-iron pan (such as a small pan in a big one), line the bigger one with a cloth to prevent scraping. I make a sack of cotton duck for each piece of cast iron gear; they get dirty and sooty and greasy, but the seasoning remains safe. Avoid cooking acidic ingredients such as tomatos in cast iron, because they can break the seasoning. It is okay to fry tomatos in cast iron, but wipe the pan out and cook something greasy right after, or wipe it with grease and burn it in. Such dishes as spaghetti sauce should be cooked in the dutch oven, where seasoning is not so important, or better, in a stainless steel pot.

Utensils

You will need a spoon, fork, ladle and spatula. They should be made of wood, nylon or plastic if you use cast iron cookware. Otherwise, stainless steel is best because it is easier to clean. If you are cooking over a campfire, long handles will bu much more comfortable. Campfires put out a lot more heat than camp stoves set to the same cooking temperature. If you use short-handle utensils, you will need to wear long sleeves and gloves while cooking.

About Food

You do not need refrigeration, but you should keep food fairly cool. That means out of direct sunlight, and not in a closed container that is in direct sunlight. A large waterproof container such as a 5-gallon plastic drum can be set in a stream and weighted with rocks to keep things cool. Tie a rope to it and to something on the bank to make sure you do not lose it. In bear country, be sure it is bear-proof. In deserts, dig a hole and bury it under 8 inches of sand, preferably in a shady spot. Drinks can be chilled by wrapping them in absorbent cloth such as a t-shirt or washcloth and keeping the cloth wet. In half an hour or so, it should be nicely cool.

Storing Food in Camp

In bear country, a solid and thick metal container will do, but many bears have learned that jars and cans, especially aluminum, might contain food. (It's actually pretty funny to watch a bear knock a beer can around, then bite it and lick up the beer, but it can also be dangerous.) Most ice-chests are *not* bear-proof. If a campground has iron food boxes, use them. Put in all food, and anything that smells of food, including clothes and toothpaste. Never keep food or anything that smells of food in your tent, for

The Lonesome Hillbilly

the bears will come right in to get it. When you hang a food sack from a tree, choose a site at least one hundred feet downwind of your camp, so when a bear comes to investigate it, it will not pass through your camp.

Wild animals want your food, and can be pretty darn clever at getting it. Their sense of smell is acute, and if they can smell food, they will try to get to it. Plastic and cloth bags are no protection. Sealed cans and glass jars are safe, except from bears and ravens. Many bears have learned that cans contain food, and can be bitten through to get at it. Some ravens know that a glass jar contains food, and how to break them open. Bears can also break into plastic coolers, and can break car windows to get inside; I have not seen any who could open a car door, but it would not surprise me. Things that do not smell of food can be kept out of sight in your tent, but everything else must be unreachable. This includes clothes that have food odors clinging to them, and toothpaste, scented oils, anything, food or not, that smells tasty. All such things, plus actual food such as bread, cookies, fresh vegetables, etc., must be kept in a strong latched metal container, or out of reach. The trunk of a car is good, and ammo cans. Many campgrounds in bear country have iron lockers for storing food.

The best storage is a large cloth bag hung out of reach. You can use just a single rope over a branch, with the rope ends tied together. If you do, hauling the food up can be difficult due to friction; a rope tossed over a branch can be impossible to move when you are trying to hoist a heavy bag. Friction can also prevent the bag from coming down. One reason for tying the ends of the ropes together is so you can haul a stuck bag down; the other is to prevent the rope end slipping over the branch and falling off. Passing a second rope through a caribiner or a small pulley makes lifting the bag easy.

If you are not in bear country, a light hammock can be strung between trees or a pair of ramada posts about four feet off the ground and at least two feet from any picnic table or tree branch. Food can be laid in it like on a shelf, and squirrels and raccoons will not be able to reach it. Ravens can still get at it, though, so keep everything covered.

In bear country, hang your food bag at least one hundred feet from your camp, and downwind so a bear scenting it will not walk through your camp to find it. The best hang is a tree with a strong branch at least fifteen feet above the ground, strong enough to not bend under the weight of your food bag when it is hung five feet from the trunk. Toss your rope over, then tie a loop in one end and tie the other end to the loop, in case the end gets stuck out of reach. Attach a caribiner clip to the loop. Pass a small rope through the clip, or through a pulley attached to the clip, and tie a loop in one end. Tie the other end of the rope to the loop so you cannot lose the rope end. With the larger rope, haul the pulley up as high as you can, then tie it off.. Attach the cloth bag to the smaller rope (the one that passes through the pulley) and haul the bag up as high as you can. The bottom of the bag should be twelve feet above the groud, and the sides of the bag should be five feet from the nearest tree trunk. The bag should hang at least two feet below the branch to discourage squirrels.

If no suitable tree is available, you can pass a rope between two trees at least twelve feet apart. Tie a loop in the middle of a 3/8 inch or larger rope and attach a caribiner clip for the hoist rope, as described above. Toss the larger rope over a small branch at least twenty feet up, so that the rope lies next to the trunk. Tie this end to the trunk. Toss the other end over a similar branch on the second tree. Haul both ends of the rope to position the loop halfway between the trees, and pull the rope as tight as you can. Secure the ends to the trunks of the trees. Keep in mind that the weight of the food bag will cause the rope to sag, so pick high enough branches to keep the bottom of the bag at least twelve feet above the ground.

Use a caribiner clip to attach your food bag to the loop in the hoist rope, and raise the bag to about two feet below the branch or horizontal rope. If the bottom of the bag is at least twelve feet above the ground and at least five feet from the nearest trunk, bears cannot get at it. When the bag is two feet below the branch or horizontal rope, squirrels *may* be able to get to it, but I have never know one to be able to chew into the sack as they can when the sack is on a table.

If you are not in bear country, you can hang the food bag in camp, and a six foot height is sufficient. Still, keep it four feet from the tree, and two feet below the branch, to frustrate the squirrels and raccoons.

Animals will chew through cloth or plastic to get at food. Ravens are smart. I have seen them open velcro closures and even zippers. Outside of bear country, you can keep food in your tent, but I advise against it. If you do, keep it away from the sides. I have had rodents chew through the tent fabric to get at dried beans that lay against the tent wall. Also keep the tent door closed, at least at the bottom, for animals will climb in looking for food. You might wake up in the night to a mouse crawling across you. Some raccoons know tents may contain food, and they are smart enough to tear their way in.

You can get a 5-gallon plastic bucket such as paint comes in, and a screw-on lid for it. This is an excellent container for bread, crackers, eggs and other "delicate" food items. Tie a rope net around it and sling it on top of your load when you travel. It can be hung from a tree or buried or set in a stream just as it is.

Spoilage

How long foods will keep depends largely on the temperature. 35 to forty degrees is just like being in a refrigerator. Sub-freezing is just like being in a freezer. Direct sunlight or 100-plus degrees spoils food quickly. Cooked meat and vegetables will keep for a couple of days *if* they are thoroughly cooked, kept cool, and in an airtight container. Cooking slightly spoiled food will kill the bacteria, but will not help the taste, and will not destroy many toxins produced by spoilage. Also, different people have different tolerances. Food that would make you sick, I could likely eat with no ill effects.

Foods that spoil quickly: use at once:
Raw chicken, fish (cooked or raw), raw pork, organ meats such as liver

Foods that keep for several days:
Beef, lamb, cooked chicken, ham, bacon, cold cuts, deli meats, hard-boiled eggs, non-pork sausages, cooked pork sausages, cooked beans, soups and stews.

Foods that keep for several weeks:
Raw eggs, if kept dry
Mayonnaise needs to be kept cool, and will keep for as much as a month, so the size of jar you get depends on how much you will use in a month.

Food that keeps a long time:
Ghee (clarified butter), dried anything, dry gains and beans, sealed cans and jars, corn meal, flour, pasta, dry mixes such as biscuit and pancake, honey and syrups, dry milk if kept in an airtight container, dried spices, opened condiments such as mustard, ketchup, jelly and jam, peanut butter

Dry Stuff

Pre-mixes are good for biscuits and pancakes, but bannock bread made from scratch is better than any biscuits I have ever had. For most things, it is better to carry scratch ingredients, because you can make everything from them, and end up carrying less weight. There are exceptions: Krusteaz pancake mix makes superb pancakes, and all you add is water. There are instant sauce and gravy mixes that weigh little and are quite tasty; my favorites are McCormick. Freeze-dried foods can be very good, but they are usually expensive, and some taste pretty poor. If water is plentiful, they can be a good choice, but if you have to carry the water for them, there is not much point.

Sandwiches are a staple when camping. When you carry a lunch on a hike, it is almost always a sandwich. But a loaf of bread is difficult to carry, because it squashes so easily, and it is the prime target of pillaging animals. A good alternative is flour tortillas. A tortilla is about the same as two slices of bread, in weight, cost and nutritional value. It is also more useful. Any sandwich you make between two slices of bread can be made by rolling the insides in a tortilla. Well, maybe not a toasted cheese. You can also roll up a lot of other things, and you can include more filling than you can between a pair of bread slices. They also allow variety. Bacon and eggs and hash browns with toast make a good breakfast. Bacon and eggs and hash browns rolled in a tortilla make the same breakfast, but it tastes very different. I use both bread and tortillas.

Salt, Pepper and Spices
Salt is necessary, especially in hot areas; always carry it. The others are luxuries, but they make such a difference in foods that I think it well worthwhile to carry a small amount of your favorites. Get small lightweight jars.

Bisquick
Makes excellent biscuits and breads, can be used to make gravy frying batter and to dredge meats, and to make pancakes and shortbread.

Krusteze Buttermilk Pancake Mix
My favorite. Makes great pancakes, and you only add water. Also good for gravy, batter and dredging.

Baking Powder
Must have for bannock and many other breads. Do not use baking soda, as it will give an unpleasant flavor if not countered by an acid such as lemon juice or cream of tartar.

Dry Bouillon
Cubes or powder. Use for making broth, gravy, or adding flavor to soups and stews.

Dry Milk
Non-fat keeps longer. Very useful. Get the kind that comes in 1-quart packets, because an opened packet will absorb humidity and become rock hard. Use in any recipe requiring milk, such as bannock bread or pancakes or biscuits from scratch. I have never found a brand that makes good milk for drinking.

I always carry flour and cornmeal, and at least three days' worth of canned goods, for times when I cannot cook (fires and stoves forbidden, high winds and high fire danger, long and heavy rain). You do not need to carry much food, since there is usually a food store nearby, so don't overburden yourself with a two-month supply!

Vitamins
I carry C, mostly for cold prevention. If you eat a varied diet of mostly fresh food, you should get all of the vitamins you need.

Recipes

Okay, I did promise you a couple of recipes.

Bannock
This is the very best camp bread, and can only be made properly on a campfire. The smoke is part of it.

1 cup flour, 1 Tbsp baking powder, 1/2 tsp salt. You can add 1 Tbsp dry milk, and 1 1/2 Tbsp fat; bacon grease is best, butter, olive oil and lard also work well. Mix the dry ingredients well, then add the fat and mix it in well. Gradually add 3/4 to 1 cup water or milk till the batter is just thin enough to run slowly. It is not critical, thin or thick, it will still bake well; none of the measures is really precise. Place it in a slightly hot cast iron fry pan and cook till a light brown crust forms on the bottom, then flip it and cook till done, OR, cook till the batter does not run when you tilt the pan 45 degrees, then place the pan next to the fire with the batter tilted towards the fire and cook till the top is just light brown. The latter method is preferred; it flavors the bread with smoke, so only use it if you have tasty smoke. The smoke from fat pine or from lumber doesn't taste so good.

As described above, this is *the* best bread for biscuits and gravy. It is also delicious just as it is, no butter needed, especially when hot from the pan. It is also a universal base; add anything you like. It takes spices very well, such as cinnamon, cardamom, paprika, just about anything. A few raisins or currants or other fruit, perhaps with a bit of sweetening, makes it a dessert. Brown sugar and cinnamon makes it coffee cake. Bits of cooked meat or fish, perhaps peas and carrots, make an excellent lunch meal for hiking. Pour half the batter in the pan, add a fried egg or two, then the rest of the batter. It is universal; use your imagination.

Corn Bread

Basically the same as Bannock Bread, but with corn meal instead of flour.

Mix 1 cup corn meal, 1/2 tsp salt and 1 Tbsp baking powder, then add 1 Tbsp lard or other fat (bacon fat is best) and mix it in well. Add 3/4 cup water and mix well. It should be just a little runny. Grease a cast iron fry pan and heat it. Add the batter and spread it about 1/2 inch thick. Put it over the fire and cook it till the bread forms a dry crust on the bottom. Loosen it with a spatula if it will not shake free. The prop the frying pan close to the fire so the bread faces the fire, or flip it over in the pan. The first way will tend to flavor the bread with smoke. Bake till the top is lightly browned (if next to the fire), or till the bottom is browned if you flipped it in the pan.

You can add goodies to the batter, such as peppers, onion, spices, etc. Vegetables can be raw or sauteed.

Steamed Rice

You need two pots, a smaller one that will be no more than 2/3 full when the rice and water have been added, and a larger one, taller and at least 2 inches wider. Both need lids. Put a trivet or a handful of pebbles in the larger pot, so the smaller one will not rest on the bottom. Add enough water to float the small pot, but not so much that the small pot can tip over. In addition, add the amount of water you will need for the rice. In the smaller pot, put the rice and any salt or spices you want. Put the larger pot on the fire to boil.

If you want the rice to be not sticky, rinse it till the water stays clear. You do not need to use purified water, unless the water contains poisons; the cooking will kill any bacteria.

When the water is boiling, dip out enough for the rice (1 1/2 cups water to each cup of rice) and add it to the smaller pot. Put the lid on the pot and place it inside the larger pot, and put the lid on that. Keep the water in the larger pot at a slow simmer, you do not need a rolling boil, and add more hot water as needed. Cook for 35 minutes for white rice, 60 for brown.

The beauty of this system is that you cannot burn or scorch the rice, and overcooking ten or fifteen minutes does no harm.

Corn Meal Mush
Use the same procedure as for Steamed Rice (above). To one cup of corn meal, add one cup of boiling water. Mix well to get rid of any lumps. Add four more cups of boiling water, and salt to taste. You can also add flavorings, such as spices, brown sugar, chopped peppers or crumbled bacon. Cover and put the small pot in the big one and cook for 20 to 25 minutes.

You can eat it hot like oatmeal, with or without milk, or let it cool, then slice it and fry the slices in butter or bacon grease. Yum!

Apple Topping (for pancakes, etc.)
Core three apples (Granny Smith are best). Peel if you wish, then slice or chop to taste. Melt 3 Tbsp butter in a cast-iron pan then saute the apples till they are not quite tender. Add 1/4 cup water, 1/3 cup dark brown sugar (more or less to taste)and 1-2 tsp cinnamon. Simmer, stirring, till as thick as you like. Pour over pancakes, or whatever. You can substitute strawberry, blueberry, orange, whatever fruit you like for apples; or white sugar, corn syrup, honey, any sweetener, or none. Try a bit of chili pepper!

Black-Eye Peas, or any dry beans
Put the black-eyes in a pot of water with lots of water and let it sit overnight, and in the sun all morning. 5 or 6 hours before dinner,

drain and rinse the black-eyes, then put them in a pot, preferably a dutch oven, with plenty of water, about 2 or 3 times the depth of the black-eyes. Put the pot on a brisk fire. For each pound of black-eyes, chop up a 12 ounce pack of bacon and a large onion. Add these to the pot with salt and pepper (go heavy on the pepper). Bring it to a boil, then move the pot to keep a slow simmer, and cover the pot. Stir occasionally and add water as needed. About 1/2 hour before dinner, you can add 1/2 cup of rice per pound of dried black-eyes, or more, up to a cup if you prefer. When done it should have the consistency of thick gravy.

Grilled Cheese Sandwiches
Slice, chop or crumble enough cheese. Take about two tablespoons of sauerkraut per sandwich, rinse it and pat it dry. In a medium hot cast-iron pan, place two slices of bread. While they are toasting, butter the upper side very lightly. When they have browned to your taste, remove them. Spread a thin layer of mayonnaise on the browned side of one slice and return it to the pan. Spread the sauerkraut on it, then cheese. Spread mayonnaise or mustard on the browned side of the other slice and place it on top of the cheese. When the bread has browned to your taste, flip the sandwich and brown the other side.

Use whatever cheese you like; I prefer extra sharp cheddar. You can replace the mayonnaise or mustard with more butter. You can also add other goodies, such as canned corned beef, lunch meat, tomato, lettuce, onion, peppers, whatever. However you do it, you get a cheap and easy meal. It is especially comforting with tomato soup on a cold drizzly day.

Beef & Beans
Take 1 pound of beef and slice it to small, thin pieces. Sautee it in 1 Tbsp butter, lard or bacon grease till it is almost done. Then add a can of pork & beans, and simmer, stirring well, till the beans are hot.

The Lonesome Hillbilly

You can use ground beef: Omit the fat and just brown it in a bare pan. You can use any kind of canned beans, but if the beans have a thin sauce, you may want to thicken it with flour or cornstarch. You can also add spice, peppers, mustard, worcestershire sauce, etc.

Simple Improvised Recipes
Heat up V8 juice and simmer till you like the thickness. Call it tomato soup. Excellent with grilled cheese sandwiches.

Prepare a package of dried gravy. Pour it over bread, rice, potatos, corn flakes.

Open a can of Dinty Moore Stew, or any soupy food, leaving about one inch of the lid uncut. Fold the sides of the lid up to a ninety degree angle, then open the lid all the way to use it as a handle. Heat the stew over the fire, then serve it in bowls, or eat it right from the can.

Any recipe can be adapted easily to the campfire, as long as it is not too precise. No "bake at 227 degrees for two minutes thirty-three seconds". You can make sophisticated dishes, but there are many very simple ones. You can spend all day cooking, or just a few minutes. Use your imagination, adapt what you have. You know the basics; that is all you need except a bit of experience.

You can also find some very good recipes in old (19th century) cookbooks, such as The Golden Age Cook Book, A Plain Cookery Book for the Working Classes, Pennsylvania Dutch Cooking, written when all they had was wood stoves. You can find these and other cookbooks for free download at Project Gutenberg: https://www.gutenberg.org/. The cookbooks listed and others of that time, and a great many others, can be found on the Cookery page:
https://www.gutenberg.org/wiki/Cookery_(Bookshelf).

Paying For It

However you camp, you still need money. If you are independently wealthy, from inheritance or savings or having a good pension, you are pretty well covered. Otherwise, you have to make an income. Odd jobs, day labor and such can provide what you need. Work a couple of days or a week and get enough to last a month or three. Or work through the winter and wander in spring, summer and fall. The main question is, how much do you really *need*? What are your expenses? You will need to figure them for yourself, I can only indicate what mine are, and how to figure them.

Bike Maintenance
Your bike has a recommended maintenance schedule. Stick to it. If you do not, you can count on breakdowns. Repairs can be very expensive, and maintenance is cheap. Most of the maintenance you can do yourself, as it is mostly changing fluids and filters. If you do, your only expense is the parts: oil, brake fluid, transmission fluid, spark plugs, air filters, oil filters, and so on. You will need a couple of special tools, such as an oil filter wrench and a torque wrench. You can find a small torque wrench at Harbor Freight Tools. It is cheap in price and quality, but good enough for occasional maintenance. Do not pollute the land when you do maintenance! It is a bother, but you can change oil cleanly with a couple of big trash bags and a roll of paper towels. Most places that do oil changes will dispose of your used oil for you; in some states, the law requires they do so.

I can afford to pay the professionals to do my maintenance work. It comes to about a thousand dollars for parts and labor every twelve to fifteen thousand miles, and that includes new tires. Call it eight cents per mile. You can economize by riding a shorter distance between campsites and staying longer at each.

Registration
Varies from state to state. If you are living on the road, you get to pick your state of residence. I chose Arizona. Registration is $72 for five years. Driver's license is $32 for five years.

Insurance
This is required in most states. The cost varies from state to state, and also from insurer to insurer. One that specializes in motorcycles will likely give you the best rate. Make sure they will cover you for a full year. Some require renewal every six months, and that is quite a hassle when you are a thousand miles from your post office box. You should be able to get insured for not more than $130 per year.

Gas
This is a big one, and quite variable. Gas prices are constantly changing, and your mileage will vary a lot. In the mountains, I get around 45 MPG. When going from one campsite to another, I get about 40. When I make a long passage, especially on freeways, it can drop as low as 30. In general, I use about 30 gallons a month, or about $75 worth.

Food
This is even bigger, and more variable. How often will you eat? I eat breakfast, a snack, and dinner. What will you eat, and how much? Canned food, fresh produce, lunch meat sandwiches, fast food? Try laying out menus for camping for a week, then price the foods. Say it works out as $3 per day, $21 per week, $1,100 per year. Or $10 per day, $70 per week, $3,650 per year. $15 per day, $115 per week, $5,475 per year. Big difference.

Camping Fees

Wildly variable! Depending on how you camp, this could range from nothing to over $6,000 per year. There are many places you can camp for free (Dispersed Camping, they call it). Most have time limits, generally 14 days, then you have to move to another camp. That is no problem, since if you are out here, you like to move around. Most developed campgrounds have nightly fees. National Forest campgrounds are mostly $5 to $28 (half that if you have an annual pass or a Senior Pass). State Parks run from $10 up. I do not know what private camps charge, but it is a lot. I generally do mostly National Forests for six months, half dispersed, half in campgrounds, and New Mexico State Parks for the rest. With my Interagency Senior Pass for the Forests and the $225 New Mexico Annual Camping Permit, I figure $700 for Forests, and another $700 for electric sites in the State Parks, so about $1600 per year, or $134 per month.

Replacement

Gear wears out. If your are only out for a couple of months, you may not need to replace anything. Long term, though, you will.

Clothes

Most common replacement. Learn to sew and to make patches, and you can greatly extend the life of clothes. You can also get quite good clothes very cheaply at thrift stores (and thrift stores are very common in the rural lands). Blue jeans are about the best pants there are, and last a long time.

Repairs

Hopefully you will not need any, but be ready for them. Have enough insurance or money in reserve to pay for heavy repairs or to buy a new bike. If you are camping full time, your bike is vital. If you wreck it or blow the motor, you are stuck till it is fixed or replaced. You do not have to get a good bike, just something that will do till you find a good one.

The Lonesome Hillbilly

__Notes__

Glossary

AMF Harley – From 1969 to 1981, Harley-Davidson Motorcycles was owned by American Machine and Foundry. AMF laid off the highest-paid employees and cut quality. The bikes manufactured in those years gave Harleys the reputation for "one hour of riding, one hour of wrenching". The company was bought back and restored, and is now back to producing high-quality bikes.

Bureau of Land Management (BLM) – The part of the Department of the Interior responsible for government owned land which is not designated for a specific use, such as National Forests and Parks. It does include some National Monuments, but is mostly undeveloped. Most is available for dispersed camping.

Bivy – A small tent, usually just large enough to hold a sleeping bag. Short for "bivouac".

Bungees – Ropes made of rubber bands enclosed in a cloth sheath. Also called shock cords.

Cager – A person driving a car or truck, riding in a cage as opposed to a biker riding in the open air.

Caribiner clip – A roughly oval shaped metal ring with a spring-loaded clip, patterned after a mountaineer's tool, but not as strong.

Cat-hole – A woodsman's toilet, a latrine hole dug for a single use, as opposed to a slit trench intended to be used several times.

Center of gravity – The point in a solid object at which weight is balanced in all directions, such as the center of a sphere.

Developed Campground – In National Forests, Parks and Monuments, an area designated as a campground and having varying facilities, including fire rings, picnic tables, outhouses, water, showers, electricity, dump stations, playgrounds, etc. Almost all charge fees, the amount depending on facilities available and popularity.

Dispersed Camping – Camping anyplace except in a developed campground. Restrictions vary between National Forests and in various BLM lands. You will have to check on local restrictions, on the internet and at local ranger stations.

Engine braking – Slowing the bike by cutting the throttle without disengaging the clutch. Usually you shift to a lower gear first; the lower the gear, the greater the braking effect.

Entrenching tool – A small folding shovel developed by the Army, used by soldiers to dig trenches and foxholes. It has a shovel blade and a pick blade, which fold back against the handle.

Firepit – A manufactured fire ring. Usually an iron ring of two foot diameter and a foot or two high, often on a cement slab, and with an attached movable grill. At most campgrounds, fires are only allowed within the firepits, and sticks must be short enough to fit inside.

Freeway bars – Heavy metal tubing mounted on a bike between the footrests and the front of the frame. They prevent the bike from resting on the rider's leg when he drops the bike. They also serve as a sort of half-way point to rest the bike when righting it.

Heel-Toe shift – A gear-shift lever by which the rider downshifts by pressing down with his toe, and upshifts by pressing down with his heel. Easier and faster than the old-style single lever which requires the rider to move his toe under the lever and lift up to upshift.

Jake brakes – A device for diesel motors which causes the motor to stop outputting power and act like brakes. It makes an extremely loud popping sound.

Kidney belt – A wide and tight belt that passes over the kidneys and provides back support.

Leatherman – A multi-purpose pocket tool, somewhat similar to the Swiss Army Knife, but more like a mechanic's tool kit.

LED – Light Emitting Diode. An electronic component that emits light with very little heat loss. It is far more efficient than an incandescent bulb, and popular in flashlights.

Low-side – Dropping a motorcycle by allowing the front tire to skid out from under while the bike is turning.

Microclimate – The weather conditions in a specific small area, such as a mountain valley, which can be very different from those in a neighboring valley.

Moment arm – Leverage. The ratio of the distances from the fulcrum between a force at one end and the load on the other. For example, if there is a one pound load one foot from the fulcrum, it takes a one pound force one foot from the fulcrum to move it, but only a half pound force two feet from the fulcrum.

Road gremlins – Gremlins are mischievous creatures who like to get into machinery and mess it up. Road gremlins dig the potholes in roads. When they get into a vehicle, they cause breakdowns. Bikers prevent this by hanging a small bell low on the bike frame. This attracts gremlins, who crawl in and get driven insane by the ringing, lose their grips, and fall to the road.

Sissy bar – A backrest on the passenger seat of a motorcycle.

Slime-type sealer – A pressurized can of gunk which is injected into a flat tire through the air valve. It coats the inside of the tire and plugs the leak. It does not work on a blowout.

Slit trench – A woodsman's toilet, a latrine hole intended to be used several times.

Trucker strap – A strong strap with hooks on the ends and a ratchet or friction lock for tightening. Very strong ones are used by truckers to secure their loads.

Washboarding – a series of small ridges running perpendicular to the road, usually caused by a grader bouncing while supposedly smoothing the road. It is not too obnoxious for cars, but can bounce a bike around severely.

White gas – a generic name for fuel used for camp stoves and lanterns, usually naphtha

About the Author

The Lonesome Hillbilly is a wanderer from birth. Born in the USA, he traveled a thousand miles by his first birthday, and ten thousand by his second. He lives on a motorcycle and in a tent he made, and hasn't slept in a building since the winter of 2013. He has been in every state of the Union, plus Asia and Europe. Politically, he is a Rational Anarchist, considering Republicans to be too liberal, Democrats too conservative, and Libertarians "OK, but not enough". Spiritually, he respects all religions, and no church. You will currently find him somewhere within five hundred miles of the Rocky Mountains. Probably.

Stay Free.

www.ingramcontent.com/pod-product-compliance
Lightning Source LLC
Chambersburg PA
CBHW070345110825
30913CB00009B/916